Dedication

To Doug and Cathy Fields

From the first moment Nancie and I became an US, we have had the privilege of having you in our lives. In a world that paints marriage as an old ball and chain, you two make marriage look oh so good. Your transparency, intention, affection, and laughter are contagious. Thanks for all the vacations, long lingering meals, and taking our calls when we have yet another "how-to-do-family" emergency. You two are generous in every sense of the word and have blessed our marriage and family in ways we will not fully understand until heaven. It's with much love, laughter, and gratitude, I dedicate the hope of this book to the two of you.

Acknowledgments

To Nancie Lee "Púg" Hoblitzell Lowe

For the way you are wired, words seem silly in this context, especially since I know you aren't a words girl. So in acknowledgment for your help with this book, I here by solemnly swear to serve you in the way you love to be loved, acts of service. So for one solid year I promise to not lay one piece of clothing on the gold chair in our bedroom. Oh baby, do I know you or do I know you? Now because I'm a words guy, I have to say to you, my Púg, that you are my favorite forever and always. You grow more beautiful by the day. You are my baby-mama. You make me laugh more than anyone on the planet. You are the best one, the only one. I love our US.

To my children, who are growing into fine young men and women: Chapman, Judson, and Teddie

You bring meaning to everything, including this book. You make my life full of everything, except money. When do I love you? All the time.

To Tim Walker

This book without you would be a hot mess and still in my computer saved in six different versions. You rescued this book from my laptop. You not only organized my words, you helped me find them, trust them, and think about them in a way I could have never done without you. Your heart, head, and friendship are all over this book. I am forever grateful.

To Reggie Joiner

Since 2001, at North Point and at Orange, you have been the one who has made it possible for me to be able to solely focus on marriages. Some days I thank you for that, some days I want to hit you for that. Your hard work makes it possible for me to do mine. Much love and thanks to you.

_____

To my friends who loved me enough to read this book . . . early

I would like to thank the men and women who read the early manuscript. Your wisdom, love, and hope for marriage are all throughout this book:
Mike and Tiffany Conyers, Mike Jeffries, Scott Kedersha, John McGee, Payden Montgomery, Michael and Shamika Owens, Afton and Hudson Phillips, Stephanie and Tom Robison, Stephanie and Ryan Porter, Kenny and Elle Campbell, Evan Chasteen, and Courtney Thomas

Endorsements

"I've read a lot of marriage books and I LOVE this book. Here's how I can tell this is a great read on marriage: I have marked up every page. I believe in Ted's message. The 'Core 4 Habits' to a great marriage are practical, life-changing, affirming, and they make sense. I know Ted and Nancie, and what I appreciate most is their absolute authenticity, passion for healthy marriage, and their fun-loving attitude. Do not pass up an opportunity to read this book."

Jim Burns, President of HomeWord and author of *Creating an Intimate Marriage, Closer*, and co-author of *Getting Ready for Marriage*

"As both a leader and an author, Ted Lowe has a priceless skill: he takes something important and very meaningful and purposefully makes it FUN. That's how he approaches this book—and that's how he suggests you approach your marriage! This book is packed with game-changing and very practical advice that you will immensely enjoy to help you create a marriage that you will immensely enjoy!"

Shaunti Feldhahn, social researcher and bestselling author of *For Women Only and For Men Only*

"One of my favorite things about Ted Lowe is his commitment to helping couples do everything they can, proactively, to avoid crises or divorce. Sometimes challenges are outside of our control, but most of the time there are habits we can develop and decisions we can make to build our marriage upon a solid foundation. In *Your Best Us*, Ted helps couples develop strong habits to set them up for long-term success. *Your Best Us* is a great read for pre-marrieds, newly marrieds, or any couple who wants to grow their relationship!"

Scott Kedersha, Director of Premarital and Newly Married Ministry at Watermark Church, scottkedersha.com

---

"If you are looking for the road map to experience your happily ever after, look no further. This is the go to handbook for any couple looking for a clear cut strategy on best practices for their marriage, backed by research and founded on the timeless truths found in scripture. With practical ideas that you can plug and play in your marriage, you are sure to not only experience deeper connection, but inspire your sense of fun too!"

Casey Caston, co-founder of Marriage365.org and co-author of *Naked Dinners* and *Communication that Connects*

Your Best Us

Published by Orange, a division of The reThink Group, Inc.
5870 Charlotte Lane, Suite 300
Cumming, GA 30040 U.S.A.

The Orange logo is a registered trademark of The reThink Group, Inc.

Other Orange products are available online and direct from the publisher. Visit OrangeBooks.com and ThinkOrange.com for more resources like these.

Website addresses and other sources of information listed throughout this book are offered as resources to you. These resources are not intended in any way to be or imply an endorsement on the part of The reThink Group, nor do we vouch for their content.

Scripture marked "NIV" is taken from the Holy Bible, NEW INTERNATIONAL VERSION®. Copyright © 1973, 1978, 1984 by Biblica, Inc. All rights reserved worldwide. Used by permission.

Scripture marked "NCV" is taken from New Century Version®. Copyright © 2005 by Thomas Nelson, Inc. Used by permission. All rights reserved.

Scripture marked NLT are taken from the Holy Bible, New Living Translation, Copyright 1996. Used by permission of Tyndale House Publishers, Inc., Wheaton, Illinois 60189.

ISBN 978-1-941259-99-3

© 2016 Ted Lowe

Lead Editor: Tim Walker
Project Manager: Nate Brandt

Printed in the United States of America
First Edition 2016

1 2 3 4 5 6 7 8 9 10
11/30/16

CONTENTS

CHAPTER

Our US

Every US is unique. Every US has a story. Every US has a beginning to their story. This is ours.

I have a picture on my desk of my wife and me when we first met. If I had to use one word to describe us at that point, it wouldn't be . . .

Cute.
Young.
Fun.
Energetic.
Hopeful.
Optimistic.
Happy.
It would be . . .
Stupid.

YOUR BEST US

Yes, when we met, apparently we lost our minds.

Our US began at a large church at a student conference called "Pack Your Bags, Jesus Is Coming." Sounds romantic, right? I was a youth pastor and had taken my youth group to the conference. The speaker told everyone they had better get ready because the rapture could happen at any moment. Every kid in my youth group was terrified they were going to get left behind. (Some of them would have been.)

While I should have been comforting them, I wasn't, because I was focused on just one person out of the 800 in attendance—Nancie Hoblitzell. When I saw her, I thought, "What in the world is she doing here?" I knew of her from college because we ran in the same social circles, even though we had never talked. I was surprised to see her because . . . well, let's just say that she, like me, was not hanging out at the campus ministry clubhouse.

She was the president of her sorority and seemed to be everywhere on campus. She was pretty and loud, and in Southern sorority girl tradition, often wore a big bow in her hair. And she was always surrounded by a bunch of other loud, pretty girls with big bows in their hair. But make no mistake about it, she was queen of the bow-heads. While I was in a fraternity that socialized with her sorority, she was so out of my league. I never dreamed of talking to her.

But there we were, three years after we both had graduated, at this conference, and I'm thinking maybe I can talk to her. During those three years, my faith had become more solid, and since she was there, I was thinking that maybe hers had too. I was thinking maybe, just maybe, God could intervene on my behalf to help me finally get the nerve to speak to Nancie Hoblitzell. I spent the conference staring at her, plotting how I could bump into her in the hall.

A friend sitting next to me said, "What do you keep looking at?"
I said, "It's not what, but who."
I pointed her out, and he said, "I know her."
I said, "You are a liar."
He said, "I swear I know her. Her name is Nancie Hoblitzell.

Her brother and I were good friends in high school."
I said, "We have to bump into her in the hall."

So we did and he introduced us. I could tell after talking with her for just a few minutes that her life had changed like mine. I got her number, and I asked her out. (That was back in the day when you got numbers and asked people out.) And by nothing short of divine intervention, she said yes.

Because I didn't want to mess things up, I took her to a really expensive restaurant. But when we got to Applebee's there was a 45-minute wait.

Nancie said, "No big deal, I don't mind waiting." But the seats in the lobby were full.
She said, "Let's just sit outside." We went outside, but the benches were full there as well.
She said, "No worries, let's just sit on the curb."
The curb? I'm thinking, "Now this is a low-maintenance woman!"

So we sat on the curb, and just like that our date was off to the races. Within 15 minutes, I started doing the relational math.

Hotness + loving Jesus—no, I mean— loving Jesus + hotness
÷ the square root of sitting on the curb × smart + funny =
Wow, she might be the one.

We stayed up that night talking until 3:00 in the morning. The next day, she was all I could think about. Nancie Hoblitzell, except for her hard-to-pronounce/remember last name, was perfect. But there was just one problem: We both lived in Alabama, and I was moving to California in just two months.

But here's the great news: She was as crazy as I was. We kept dating and acting as if I weren't moving. But as the day of my move drew closer, we started asking ourselves, what are we going to do?

Our answer: Make a lifelong decision way too soon.

About a week before I was supposed to leave for California, I said to her, "I know you want to teach at a junior college, and I just happen to know that there are several junior colleges where I am moving."

She said in her oh-so-cute, perfect way, "I'm not moving to California to be your girlfriend."

And I said in my oh-so-cute, perfect way, "Then why don't you move to California to be my wife?" Boom.

So we decided to get married, to become an US. Of course we didn't share this with anyone, because it made no sense. So I moved to California. We bought many plane tickets on our credit cards to see each other, and got married exactly one year from our first date.

And there we were, newlyweds in our early 20s, living in beautiful, sunny Southern California, enjoying our great, low-paying jobs, surrounded by amazing people. Everything should have been perfect, right? It wasn't— at least not all the time.

We thought we were going to be different from other married couples. And by different, I mean great. We thought we had something special that the rest of the married population appeared not to have.
We weren't going to fight.
Our love would always find a better way.
This bliss we were experiencing would never end.
Our US was going to be beautiful in every way, unique in every way, every single moment of every single day.

Our marriage was unique, but our struggles were common. We weren't a train wreck, but on some days we got close. And on other days, we were stinking adorable. We enjoyed each other so much.

We were what we now describe as average, with moments of awesome and moments of awful.

And it was no wonder we had moments of awesome. We had quickly but unintentionally created some great marital habits:
We were both strong in our faith.
We were still silly and fun with each other.
We made time for each other.
We had sex often.
We surrounded ourselves with great people.
We both cared how we treated each other.
We spent time with another couple who modeled what it meant to have a great marriage.

These habits led us to have moments of awesome. These moments made us feel connected, in love, and in like with each other.

But we had also quickly but unintentionally created some bad marital habits that led to moments of awful. At lightning speed, we could go from feeling very connected to very disconnected. I remember thinking how crazy it was that it only took one wrong look, minor disagreement, or unmet expectation to ruin an otherwise perfectly great day. While our moments of awesome were varied in size and shape, our moments of awful had become a script we acted out over and over.

It went a little something like this: I would say something the wrong way. She would shut down. I would relentlessly try to get her to tell me what was wrong. She would finally tell me. I would then clarify in painstaking detail how she had heard me the "wrong" way.

This was our connection-killing habit, regardless of how trivial the topic. We would get amped up over petty things like what time we needed to leave, feeding the dog, taking out the trash, speaking words with a certain tone, being too quiet, being too loud, spending time with our friends, not spending time with our friends, buying this, not buying this, saying that, not saying that . . . the options were endless, but the ugly dance was basically the same.

Like our moments of awesome, it was no wonder we had moments of awful. We were very different people with different backgrounds.

Growing up, Nancie moved often due to her dad's job as a coach. My dad is a fifth-generation farmer who wasn't moving us anywhere. She had a stay-at-home mom. My mom died when I was 10. On top of that, our personalities were and are very different. We have different views on money. She has the brain of an accountant. I have a brain floating in a sea of ADHD. She is very scheduled. I am very spontaneous. So in our first few years of marriage, our differences were like relational bumper cars; some days the bumps were fun and giddy, other days they hurt.

But then our US took an unexpected twist.

Amazingly, and giving no credit to our US, we were working at one of the largest churches in the country, Saddleback Community Church, where Rick Warren is the pastor. If you haven't heard of Rick Warren, he is like the Elvis of pastors, and Saddleback Church is Graceland. I will save you the very long story of how this happened, but through a crazy turn of events, we started performing sketches and skits in the weekend worship services.

To help him make a point in his messages, Pastor Rick asked us to act out 6–10-minute scenes of a married couple experiencing the different tensions or situations he was addressing in his sermon series.

After the services, people often told us they had the exact same experiences in their own marriages. One couple even accused us and the church of spying on them. (They weren't kidding.) Married couples passionately wanted us to know that they related to what they had just seen us play out on stage. These scenes resonated so much with people that we quickly became regulars at the weekend services as well as at the marriage events at our church.

The next thing we knew, it was five years and one baby later, and we were traveling all over the country acting at different marriage and youth events. But our moments of awesome were starting to be overshadowed by our moments of awful.

As we were performing at one event, I noticed that our faces were on hundreds of screens throughout the arena. We were in front of 18,000 people, and I got a little puffed up with pride. After the performance, we were walking down the stage stairs while people were still clapping, and I said, "Wow, that was incredible." Nancie said, "I just want to get home to the baby." Why? Because just moments prior to that performance we had been fighting in the green room. It appeared that not even arena events could trump the effects of our increasing moments of awful.

But as we traveled, there was still something in me that knew our marriage could be better. I somehow knew not to settle. I became increasingly sure God didn't want us to settle either. I felt more compelled every day to figure this marriage thing out—not just for us, but also for other couples who were experiencing the same things. So I started listening to the marriage experts who surrounded us at these events. I was reading every marriage book I could get my hands on. I asked successful married couples how they did it. I became a student of marriage. I started to secretly and not so secretly implement some of my findings in our own marriage. Some of these simple changes were working. Moments of awesome in our US increased. Moments of awful in our US decreased.

I didn't want to keep this hope to myself. Just as our scenes of tension had resonated with people, I wanted to provide answers that empowered people. I wanted to help couples start to experience what we were finally experiencing. While there were many good ways to do that, for me, I felt the church was the best place to start.

So after many prayers and conversations with Nancie, I was compelled to figure out ways to help marriages through the local church. I wanted to create avenues for the local church to help marriages in a way that would resonate with women AND men. I wanted to give couples bite-size wins for their marriage instead of dumping five years' worth of content on them in two days. I wanted to do it in a way that resonated with every marriage regardless of their faith. And I wanted it to be fun. So I dreamed and wrote and had conversations and researched, and I felt in my gut that this was what I was created to do.

As we continued to travel, I met another very influential pastor of a large church—Andy Stanley, pastor of North Point Community Church in Alpharetta, Georgia. I shared with him my heart's desire to help married couples. He introduced me to the family pastor at North Point, Reggie Joiner. I shared with Reggie the same thing I had shared with Andy. Several interviews later, I was offered the job as the Director of Married Life at North Point Church. *(Record screech)*

What? We had been married six years at the time they hired me. And while we had found some hope, we were still experiencing some moments of awful. I'm not sure who was crazier—them for hiring me, or me for saying yes. Yet, I had a sense of peace (most days) and an even bigger sense of excitement (some days).

I led a team that was given the rare gift in ministry to create something that hadn't been done before. And I knew I wanted to create something not only for couples who were stuck or on the verge of divorce, but also for the countless numbers of couples like us experiencing varying moments of awesome and awful.

One of the first things we created at our church were quarterly one-night events for married couples. We worked very hard to make the events proactive, appealing to both men and women, fun, and—following Andy Stanley's message model[1]—we wanted couples to walk away with just one, doable thing that could make their marriage better. In preparation for each quarter, I would dive into a passage from the Bible that was relevant to marriage. I would study it to death, and out of that time something powerful would emerge: one simple truth with one powerful action. Here's the crazy part: Secular research also backed up these biblical principles and applications, so these truths were relevant to every person in the room.

Putting these truths into action worked not only in our own marriage but also in the marriages of the people at our church. We heard story after story of couples who were applying these simple applications to complex issues. They were experiencing wins in their marriages like never before. To the events we added small group experiences focused on marriage and date nights for couples to do on their own. So many married people were having more and more moments of awesome and fewer and fewer moments of awful. I was Director of MarriedLife for nine years before starting MarriedPeople[2], an organization with the mission to help churches help marriages. Every year we help thousands of churches teach what you are going to learn in this book.

So since 2001, my job has been to help married couples—in the real world—have a great marriage. And in the middle of pouring into other marriages all these years, I think our US has benefited the most. Nancie and I are two very stubborn, opinionated, different people. We have three kids we adore but who also serve up their own daily doses of awesome and awful. We have experienced great tragedy in our years together. But in the middle of it, we have a great marriage—not because we are perfect, but because we have applied what you are about to discover in this book.

That is why I finally decided after all these years to write this book. Because so many marriages, mine included, have practiced these easy-to-understand principles and applications, and they work.

So often in the name of helping married couples, experts with great intentions paint a picture of the perfect couple that no one can live up to. This book isn't that. This book is designed to help you become your best US.

Because there are things you like to do, places you like to go, and histories that are your own. And whether you are loving your US, wondering if your US is going to make it, or somewhere in-between, we all, at some level, want to become our best US.

And here's the great news, while the way we are wired both individually and as a couple may be different . . .
While our stage of life might be different . . .
While our situations may be different . . .

We all, at some level, want to become our best US.

There are some great marital habits that empower all of us—specifically four core habits (that come from the Bible) that can help every couple become their best US.

You can do what you are about to read even while living in the real world. So get ready, because your US isn't going to know what hit it . . . in a good way.

CHAPTER

Your Best US

What does it take?

So what does it take to have a great US?

What does it take to have a great marriage? What are the marital habits that are great for your US? Is it . . .

Hard Work?

People seemed compelled to tell engaged and newly married couples that marriage takes hard work. And they say it with a sigh. The problem is that most people can't tell you what hard work in a marriage even means. The other problem with hard work being the answer is the simple fact that most people, after a long day at work, don't want to work more. So they don't.

Communication?

Just reading the word communication in a marriage book might fill you with joy. But the problem with communication being the answer to a great marriage is that often you have one spouse in a marriage who likes to communicate, and then you have husbands. I tease. About 25 percent of the time, it is the husband who likes to talk and the wife who doesn't. Either way, communication can be tricky.

Chemistry?

When you first met, the two of you had such great chemistry. No, really, you had great chemistry—like with real chemicals. In the past decade, researchers have studied the brains of people who are in the infatuation stage[3]. One discovery was made by sending people in the infatuation stage through an MRI machine while showing them a picture of their beloved. Consistently, people's brains have the same reaction—activity in the frontal lobe decreases. The frontal lobe is where long-term reasoning and logic live. At the same time, three areas of the brain light up like a Christmas tree. These are the same three areas of the brain that light up when someone uses cocaine. So when you first got married, you weren't in love, you were stoned. Then these studies show that over time, the frontal lobe goes back to operating at pre-infatuation capacity, and the feel-good chemicals subside. Often this leaves couples wondering, "What happened?"

Compatibility?

Over the past 10–15 years, many people have found each other through online compatibility tests. Regardless if you had the chance to take a test or not, there are days—maybe even seasons—when you are not compatible, which makes compatibility a pretty weak foundation on which to base your marriage.

So what does it take to have a great US? All of the factors listed above?

Here's where my experience and research have led me. I think the answers to marriage are found in the Bible. Those answers are also amplified and clarified through research. When you dive in to see what the Bible has to say about marriage, there are not a lot of verses that have "how-tos."

The Bible also calls marriage a mystery (Ephesians 5:32 NIV). This may be the only time in the Bible where the author punts—"Oh marriage, it's a mystery."

And let's be real here . . . the Bible doesn't show us a lot of examples of marriage, and the ones it does show are often more than a little messed up. There are no perfect couples in the Bible. (There are no perfect parents either, but that's a story for another book.[4]) But there are principles in the Bible that, if applied, can change everything. If you aren't sure how you feel about the Bible, stay with me, because again, research reveals these principles as well.

So what does the Bible have to say about marriage? The four core habits in this book are based on a few passages specifically about marriage that also have action verbs in them. But before I give you those verses that describe the four habits, I want to give you a broader context.

One theme that we consistently find throughout the Bible is that every author warns readers of how culture impacts their relationships with each other and their relationship with God.

Paul, who authored much of the New Testament, wrote letters to Christians to give them a heads-up of what to look out for in their particular situation and culture. In the book of Colossians, we find the people in Colossae surrounded by two primary groups of people: those who were passionately devoted to Jewish customs and traditions, and those who were living life based on a mix of Christian principles and philosophy. So he sent them a warning:

> *See to it that no one takes you captive through hollow and deceptive philosophy, which depends on human tradition and the elemental spiritual forces of this world rather than on Christ (Colossians 2:8 NIV).*

What can take you captive? Hollow and deceptive philosophy, which depends on human traditions. In other words we, like the people in Colossae, do things because everyone around us is doing them. Much to our parents' dismay, apparently we would jump off a bridge if our friends were doing it.

- Imagine me saying this with my Southern accent: "We talk like this because this is the way our mamas and daddies talk."
- Imagine a co-worker saying this as you are racing to a meeting: "We work this way because this is how people work in our company."
- Imagine your friend saying this as you drop your kid off at _____: "We put our kids in _____ because that's what every parent does."

It's so easy for us to live without questioning much of what we do simply because it's what other people do. As in the verse above—we do it because it's *human tradition*.

This dynamic is also fueled by the elemental spiritual forces of this world. If that freaks you out, it should . . . a little. We are told there is a battle we can't see, one where good is at war with evil (Ephesians 6:12 NIV). And when we live life on culture-matching hamster wheels, we are losing the battle . . . daily. If you aren't a Christian and this sounds like spiritual mumbo jumbo, I think we can still all agree that there is a current, cultural momentum that isn't great for our marriages.

But as much as this passage points to darkness, it points to light with these four powerful words: *rather than on Christ*. Paul is encouraging us to trade in the world's way of doing life with God's way of doing life. Paul says, don't get sucked in. Don't do it just because it's what everyone else is doing. Stop. Pause. Question. Decide.

That is what this book is about: you stopping, pausing, questioning, and deciding what you want in your marriage instead of living like most married couples. It's about developing the right marital habits.

And as I said in chapter one, these new habits aren't many and they aren't complex. My friend, Dr. Jeff Fray, who is also a psychologist, puts it this way:

"We have convinced a generation that a group of Ph.D.s like me have tucked away the difficult secrets to marriage, and that the average Joe-and-Sue married couple has to somehow extract and interpret those secrets. Most couples have just forgotten the basics, like being kind."

Consistently loving our spouse in the simple ways God directs us to love them, creates great marriage habits. And while every US is different, these habits lead people of all different backgrounds and situations to connect.

Consistently loving our spouse in the simple ways God directs us to love them creates great marriage habits.

And if you are not sure how you feel about God or the Bible guiding your marriage, I think we can all agree on this point:

Your marital habits either lead to the connection
or the disconnection of your US.

How does that sentence sit with you? For many of us, it leaves us feeling discouraged. We have other habits we have tried to change and have been unsuccessful, i.e., exercising, reading vs. watching TV, eating healthier, staying organized. But marital habits are different because they're relational. They're relational, which means they're emotional, and therein lies the answer.

Great habits happen in the midst of emotion = moments of awesome.
Bad habits happen in the midst of emotion = moments of awful.

So by emotion, do I mean the ooey-gooey, look-into-each-other's-eyes moments? Do I mean those times when you are both angry and say those things you wish you had never said? While those times can be part of marriage, for most it is a very, very small percentage of our US. What I'm talking about is the majority of everyday interactions we have with our spouse. It's during those simple daily exchanges that we see the power of great marital habits.

For instance, here are a few examples of small but huge emotional moments.

- When you decide to laugh off something trivial instead picking a fight, that is emotional. That matters.
- When you choose to be tender when you want to be harsh, that is emotional. That matters.
- When you thank your spouse for providing for the family, that is emotional. That matters.
- When you pick up the kids at school even when it's not your turn, that is emotional. That matters.
- When you pause in the morning to pray for your spouse, that is emotional. That matters.

Why do these emotional moments matter? Charles Duhigg, researcher and author, says that our habits become more flexible during times when we are emotional.[5] Marriage at its very core is emotional. Marital moments evoke emotion; we just have to learn how to leverage those emotions, even create those emotions, to help us connect instead of disconnect.

But strides in marriage don't typically happen with a big explosion of growth. In my own marriage, it has been slow growth. But I will say small acts of kindness have been remarkable for our US almost from the moment we first tried them. And stopping the bad habits of our US have impacted our marriage even more quickly.

For almost every couple, an unexpected moment of laughter, gentleness, respect, affirmation, and/or sexual connection can often trigger a great day for your marriage, even in the toughest of situations. And we can choose to create those moments in our marriage.

You may be thinking, "We are way past this point of the 'small things equal big things mentality.' We have huge issues." You could be right. If you are struggling with issues like infidelity or abuse, you need to seek help. Call a counselor or a pastor. But most marriages don't break apart from the "biggies." Most dissolve slowly over time through bad marital habits.

Maybe your bad marital habits have led you to start thinking, "We are just another couple who isn't going to make it. We are just another sad statistic." But no matter how many people get a divorce, it is no less painful for all involved.

Here's the counter and the hope to the "we're just another sad stat" philosophy: **Your marriage is not a statistic; it's a story**. Your habits—not data about other couples—determine the story your US is telling. And the hope lies in the fact that you can choose the best habits to write the best story, no matter the condition of your US. That's why we are going to take a look at just four habits that work in the real world of real couples who have different levels of satisfaction with their US.

We call these habits the . . .

CORE 4 HABITS OF A GREAT MARRIAGE

We are going to focus individually on each of the Core 4 Habits, but first I want to give you a preview of where we are headed.

The first Core 4 Habit is **Have Serious Fun**. We can get so serious with all the "important" things in our lives, but we will discover why having serious fun is a must for every marriage.

The second Core 4 Habit is **Love God First**. We are going to take a look at how God fits into your marriage, and I think the answer may surprise you. The third Core 4 Habit is **Respect and Love**. In every marriage, there is a cycle of respect and love. By understanding this cycle, we start to understand how to increase the times we feel connected and decrease the times we don't.

The fourth and final Core 4 Habit is **Practice Your Promise**. On your wedding day, you probably promised your spouse some pretty big things. We will explore how to live out those big promises in small ways that really matter.

Now, I'm in no way saying these habits are the only way to have a great marriage. But I am saying that consistently loving our spouse God's way creates great habits. And while every US is unique, these Core 4 Habits lead couples from different backgrounds and situations to connect in a way they might never have thought possible.

So no matter where you are in your marriage, I want to give you a challenge. Give these Core 4 Habits a try by practicing each one for seven days before moving on to the next habit. They are not a quick fix, and like any other habit, they take time and intention to become consistent in your life. But they offer almost any marriage great hope to start heading or stay headed in the right direction.

To make these habits super practical, in each chapter you will find a MAKE IT A HABIT section for one of the Core 4 Habits. From there you are encouraged to practice the habit in very specific ways for seven days. Then you can move onto the next chapter.

Finally, whatever the reason you are reading this book, I have a common prayer and focus for all of us, and it comes from a passage that I landed on when I first started working with married couples. It has been my goal ever since. Paul wrote in Colossians 2:2-3:

WHAT DOES IT TAKE?

*My goal is that they may be **encouraged in heart** and **united in love**,*
so that they may have the full riches of complete understanding, in
order that they may know the mystery of God, namely, Christ, in whom
are hidden all the treasures of wisdom and knowledge
(NIV, emphasis added).

Yes, my goal—but much more importantly, God's goal—for you is that you would be encouraged in heart and united in love. How? By applying to your marriage the habits that come from God's hidden treasures of wisdom and knowledge.

So whether you are loving your US, wondering if your US is going to make it, or somewhere in-between, these Core 4 Habits can help you become your best US.

YOUR BEST US

CHAPTER

Your Best Us

Have Serious Fun

If someone had asked you before you got married if you wanted your future spouse to be fun, what would you have said?

For most of us, the quick answer would have been "Yes!"

For Nancie and me, it would have been a big "YES!"

And despite our moments of awful in our first few years of marriage, we had some moments of awesome that often involved fun. We would go to the beach, usually on Saturdays, which we loved because it was not only beautiful and relaxing, it was free.

And fun for our US wasn't reserved for the weekends. On any given day of the week, I would do silly things at home just to get a fun reaction out of her—like at random times I would walk out wearing my scuba diving skins. On Tuesdays, we went to the "cheap" movies. Our sex life was fun, creative, and happened on a very regular basis. We did unexpected things like writing love notes on the bathroom mirror in lipstick and shaving cream. We took time to linger and to laugh, to have fun.

In the beginning of our marriage, I was fun. She was fun. We made time for fun.

Today, I am still fun. She is still fun. We still make time for fun. And I don't say that to boast or make you feel bad if you are not having fun in your marriage. I say it because fun is much of what makes my marriage to Nancie not perfect, but rich and solid. I say it because I want every married couple to make time for fun, because it matters much more than many of us realize.

But is fun really essential for your marriage, or is it simply extra? Sure, we all like fun. But it's easy to think that other things in our lives are more important than having fun as a couple—like bills, kids, and chores. Maybe you've never thought about the importance of fun in your marriage. Why should you? After all, so few of us have people or things that tell us fun is an important element of marriage. And there are even fewer people and things that prompt us to actually have fun. Fun in our marriage can be difficult, because there are so many hurdles to our fun. Here are some common fun barriers.

Fun Barrier #1: Busyness
Let's state the obvious: Most of us are too busy. Our lives are filled with have-tos. Think about how many times you start sentences with,
"I have to_____."
"I have to pick up my kid from soccer practice."
"I have to get ready for tomorrow's meeting."
"I have to take my mom to the doctor."
"I have to do the laundry."

We can get so busy that we don't even think about fun. And even if we do think about it, we typically don't toy with the idea long enough to actually do anything about it. There are just so many things we have to do.
The have-tos seem bigger than fun.

Fun Barrier #2: Seriousness

Married people can be some seriously serious people. And why shouldn't we be serious? We have mortgages, jobs, kids, aging parents, chores, etc., etc., etc. We become serious because we have seriously important people and things in our lives. There are people depending on us. And while these things are obviously of great importance, they can also begin to take the life out of our US.

Serious focus on what is seriously important seems bigger than fun.

Fun Barrier #3: Children

If you're a parent, you love your kids. Oh, how we love them. So we put them first. But let's be honest, kids can take a toll our marriages. Kids are marital suckerfish. It is so easy to center our lives on their needs, wants, and activities. So we put off fun until later. We tell ourselves once the kids are older or out of the house, then we will take time for the two of us. Then the kids move out and we look across the table at our spouse and think, "Who are you?"

Our children having what they "need" seems bigger than fun.

Fun Barrier #4: Exhaustion

We don't make time for fun as a couple because often we are simply too tired. We are too exhausted to be fun people. Even if we do make time for fun, we are not sure we could have any because we are so drained. With everything else going on in our world, it is easy to feel like we don't have the energy or words to have fun.

Exhaustion seems bigger than fun.

Fun Barrier #5: Uncertainty

Some of us are unsure what fun even means anymore. We wonder, "What if I try to be funny around the house and I'm not funny? What if we go out and it's not fun? What if I was never funny? What if we have become one of those couples in restaurants who say nothing and do nothing except look at their phones? What if we start talking about something other than work and the kids and we realize we have nothing in common, no ability to communicate? What if we realize we have some serious issues? Shouldn't we just leave well enough alone?"

So many, many things seem bigger than fun.

You may be thinking that so many things seem so much more important than fun, and they are important. But hang with me for just a few pages as I try to convince you that fun in a marriage isn't extra, it's essential.

The verses I want to share with you come from Proverbs 5 and are written by Solomon. Solomon asked God for one thing: wisdom. And God gave it to him.

Fun in a marriage isn't extra, it's essential.

That God-given wisdom is recorded in the book of Proverbs. Solomon's wisdom is not based on his human ability. In fact, Solomon's own life wasn't a great example of marriage. He had many wives and concubines. But the principles and the truths that God spoke through Solomon are ones we can all strive to live by.

These verses will not only paint the picture of the importance of fun, sex, and intimacy, they can help you protect your marriage from the most serious of issues, even the big ones . . . like adultery.

Whoa, hold on! We were just talking about fun and now you drop the "a" word. Yes, ironically enough, this seemingly light habit of having serious fun comes from a heavy passage. But that's actually fantastic, because it shows us that having serious fun is essential and simply can't wait. This should actually get us excited, because fun should be one of the greatest parts of our marriage.

In these verses Solomon is warning his son to protect himself and his marriage by staying away from adultery. But this passage can also be applied to other things that are destructive to our lives, like the constant pursuit of power and possessions. For 14 verses, Solomon tries to scare the pants *on* his son. I know 14 verses is a lot, but please read them all. If nothing else, it's some juicy reading, and some of the verses read like tag lines to horror films, especially verse 5 (which I've bolded below for emphasis).

> *My son, pay attention to my wisdom, turn your ear to my words of insight, that you may maintain discretion and your lips may preserve knowledge. For the lips of the adulterous woman drip honey, and her speech is smoother than oil; but in the end she is bitter as gall, sharp as a double-edged sword. **Her feet go down to death; her steps lead straight to the grave.** She gives no thought to the way of life; her paths wander aimlessly, but she does not know it.*

> *Now then, my sons, listen to me; do not turn aside from what I say. Keep to a path far from her, do not go near the door of her house, lest you lose your honor to others and your dignity to one who is cruel, lest strangers feast on your wealth and your toil enrich the house of another. At the end of your life you will groan, when your flesh and body are spent. You will say, "How I hated discipline! How my heart spurned correction! I would not obey my teachers or turn my ear to my instructors. And I was soon in serious trouble in the assembly of God's people" (Proverbs 5:1–14 NIV, emphasis added).*

Solomon's passionate warning about adultery actually brings something great to the surface: It speaks to the fact that most of us are designed to crave a deep emotional and sexual relationship with one other person. This craving is a beautiful thing and part of a great marriage. But here is the catch: This craving doesn't take a vacation; it's always with us, in us.

It goes to work with us.
It goes to the gym with us.
It goes to the cul-de-sac with us.
It goes online with us.
It's in us when we are with our spouse, and when we are not.

Now, I'm not saying we should be scared of this huge desire; I'm saying we should respect it. And most of all, we should enjoy it—with our spouse. This is what Solomon instructs his son and us to do in these next few verses. He says:

> *Drink water from your own cistern, running water from your own well. Should your springs overflow in the streets, your streams of water in the public squares? Let them be yours alone, never to be shared with strangers. May your fountain be blessed, and may you rejoice in the wife of your youth. A loving doe, a graceful deer—may her breasts satisfy you always, may you ever be intoxicated with her love.*
> *(Proverbs 5:15–18 NIV).*

So if you thought the Bible was boring, now you know better.

How do you protect your marriage from other love affairs? Enjoy your marriage. In fact, **one of the best ways to protect your marriage is to enjoy your marriage.**

One of the best ways to protect your marriage is to enjoy your marriage.

This great need to connect with and enjoy each other—to Have Serious Fun—is not extra, it's essential. That's why this core habit isn't simply called Have Fun. We must have SERIOUS fun because fun can't wait; it's serious. This is really good news because it's what we hoped for before we were married, and I believe it's what many of us still long to have in our US. Fun is the good stuff of marriage. And fun is essential to our marriage.

Solomon ups his game: *May her breasts satisfy you always, may you ever be intoxicated with her love* (v. 15). God wants our marriages to be consistently rich, sexy, and intimate to the point of two people becoming one person. That's amazing. God wants us to rejoice, to have fun with our wife/husband—the one we promised we would radically love for the rest of our lives.

God wants us to rejoice in our marriages. God wants our marriages to be so great that we are intoxicated with our spouse's love, intoxicated with each other's love.

I know for some, actually for a lot of us, that's a pretty lofty goal. Especially if you are in a spot where you might settle for descriptors like "tolerate my spouse's love." You may be thinking words like *intoxicated* are feeling words, and you can't make yourself feel something you don't. But this isn't an issue of feelings; it is an issue of focus.

This is about focusing your heart and this deep craving towards your spouse. When you do, the feelings often follow. But no matter how you would rank your marriage, God has put in you a desire to have something deeply beautiful with your spouse. And when this is lacking in our marriage, on a subconscious or even conscious level, we know it. It's one of the reasons you are reading this book. This deep desire in you is part of the push for you to want something more for your marriage—more sex, more intimacy, more joy, more fun.

And research is unveiling the same truths. John Gottman, Ph.D., a leading marriage researcher, states: "Marriage isn't just about raising kids, splitting chores, and making love. It can also have a spiritual dimension that has to do with creating an inner life together—a culture rich with symbols and rituals, and appreciation for your roles and goals that link you, that lead you to understand what it means to be part of the family you have become."[6]

He goes on to say, "In essence, each couple and each family create its own microculture. And like other cultures these small units have their customs (like Sunday dinner out), rituals (like a champagne toast after each birth of a baby), and myths—the stories the couple tell themselves (whether true, false, or embellished) that explain their sense of what their marriage is like, what it means to be part of their group."

In other words, happy couples make time for each other. They have things they love to do as an US. It's true. Think about it: What do most couples say after having a great time with their spouse?

They say, "We should do *that* more often."

Don't miss the power of the word "that" in the previous sentence. Because . . .
- "That" is where we laugh.
- "That" gives us a break from stress and worry.
- "That" is what is important at the end of our lives.
- "That" gives us something to draw from when things get tough.
- "That" is where fun lives.
- "That" is the background for our US to connect.

At the risk of being dramatic, our very souls seem to be screaming that we need more of "that" fun stuff.

But how do we have fun as a married couple in the real world, a world that is full of fun barriers—barriers that are not optional, like work and kids?

How Do We Have Serious Fun?
Let's start by stating what fun is not. Fun, despite the depictions in stock photography, is not perfect-looking couples doing impossible-looking things in expensive-looking locations. I feel quite sure if I tried to ride a bicycle with my wife on the handlebars going down a winding road in Hawaii, one or both of us would die, or at the very least knock out our front teeth. Yes, fun looks different for every US. But fun doesn't require perfection. Fun requires participation. So how do us mere mortals have fun with our spouse?

Be Fun

Let's start with being fun. I am a huge proponent of date nights and special times for couples. And we will talk about that later in the chapter. But what's even better than a fun date night is a fun life, a life filled with a let's-not-take-ourselves-so-seriously tone. Is your tone too serious? Do you forget to turn off your, what my wife calls "work voice"?

We need to be intentionally fun when we are together at home, when we text or call each other, or wherever we may be. It's important to make what you are already doing fun.

Fun doesn't require perfection. Fun requires participation.

- Make dinner more fun by turning off the TV and cooking together.
- Turn on music you used to listen to when you were dating and make out in front of the kids until one or all of them screams, "That's disgusting!" Then kiss for 30 more seconds.
- String Christmas lights up in your bedroom . . . in July.
- Watch some goofy YouTube videos.
- Leave funny and sexy Post-It® notes for each other.
- Send some silly or sexy texts in the middle of the day.
- Leverage sarcasm if you AND your spouse are both into it. One of my close friends says that in his marriage, snarkiness is their love language.
- Make an awkward family reunion fun by choosing a word you have to interject five times into conversations with relatives. I personally love the word *whippersnapper*, but feel free to choose your own. But choosing is the key.
- Make the time when you reconnect at the end of the day fun by meeting at the door and making out, dancing, etc.

Choose to be fun. Choose what is fun for your US. It only has to work for your US.

Get into the habit of fun. Then, to make sure it happens consistently schedule fun.

Yes, you read that right. You need to schedule fun. We have to make time for fun just like we make time for other things, even the things we don't want to do, like going to the doctor or soccer practice four nights a week. We have to make time to have fun as a couple. But how do we do that in the real world? Think about it—the things that happen in our lives are the things where we take the steps necessary to fill in the following five blanks:

Who   _____
What   _____
When   _____
Where   _____
How   _____

When we fill in all five blanks, we do it. So determine what you both like to do for fun, and fill in all five blanks. Do you like to ride bikes together, take walks together, eat out, shop, play tennis, binge watch a TV show? Find what you like to do as an US. Remember it only has to work for *your* US. Then do it.

For us, once all of our kids were in school, Friday mornings became the best time for us to have a date. Our US loves Friday mornings. We typically take a couple of hours to work out together or grab lunch or go to a movie or to a museum or stay home—which is my personal favorite. No kids banging on the door is amazing! In fact, we don't even have to shut the door. Friday mornings are probably out of the question for most couples, but when is it not out of the question? Be consistent with the time, but not the fun. Mix it up.

Do what is uniquely fun for your US. Go to Home Depot and talk about projects you would love to do . . . one day. Get ice cream. Go to a fancy hotel if you have the funds.

And speaking of funds, if you have to choose between material things and experiences with your spouse, social scientists say to pick experiences. Psychologists Tom Gilovich and Leaf Van Boven, pioneering researchers, state:

"Experiences are more likely to make us happy than material goods, because they bring us closer to other people . . . . Experiences are better than material goods because of something psychologists call 'positive re-interpretation,' and what you or I would call 'looking through rose-tinted glasses.' If you buy a bad material good, like shoes that hurt or trousers that make you look fat, you're stuck with the fact you made a bad choice. Those shoes will always hurt. But with experiences it's not like that. You can make them seem better in your mind."[7]

It's true for many of us. Experiences bring us together. When we think back on vacation, we don't remember the five-hour drive, we remember the time in the mountains.

What's the difference between couples who know dating is important but don't do it, and those who make it happen? Scheduled, consistent times. Now let's consider how to make having serious fun a habit.

MAKE IT A HABIT

HAVE SERIOUS FUN

For each habit, there is an exercise. Once you complete the exercise below, practice the habit for seven days. Then move to the next chapter.

To make having serious fun a habit, do the following.

Fill in the who, what, when, where, and how regarding three different ways experts suggest you can stay connected and have fun in the middle of life: schedule daily dialogue, date night, and sex.

Schedule Daily Dialogue

The average couple spends four minutes a day in meaningful conversation. Have you ever dedicated four minutes a day to something and seen it become successful? So I want to stretch you just a bit by giving you a common marriage tip. Carve out 5–15 minutes a day to talk. It may seem impossible, but it is not. You are adults; you can choose to make the time. Here's an example of how you can do it, but remember to do what works for your US.

Daily Dialogue
Example:
Who: You and your spouse
What: Talk 15 minutes

- 5 minutes to talk about necessary details of the week
- 5 minutes for your high and low of the day
- 5 minutes for your funny of the day

When: Monday–Friday at 8 p.m.
Where: In your bedroom with door closed . . . or better yet, locked
How: Put it on the calendar, and show up on time.

Now it's your turn:
Who: _____
What _____
When: _____
Where: _____
How: _____

Schedule Date Night

The second thing you need to schedule is date night.
While a weekly date night or date morning or date lunch would be ideal, you can start with bimonthly or even monthly date nights if you have to. Just start.

Now let's see what that looks like in the real world.

Date Night

Example:
Who: You and your spouse
What: Date night—dinner and some laughs
When: Thursday
Where: Whatever your favorite place of the moment is.
How: Get a babysitter and a date night. No talking about serious marital issues, kids, etc.

Now it's your turn:
Who: _____
What: _____
When: _____
Where: _____
How: _____

Schedule Sex

So where does sex fit into all this? If you are playful and fun and carving out moments for your US, then sex can be a byproduct of that. But not always. That is why so many marriage experts suggest we schedule a third thing: sex.

Some people fear that scheduling sex will take away the spontaneity of sex. I get it and I'm not suggesting sex should never be spontaneous. It should! But scheduling it never hurts, and it almost always helps. Yes, most of us need to schedule sex. Why? Because we are busy, and oftentimes if we don't schedule it, it won't happen. But maybe the most important reason to schedule sex is because in marriage you typically have one spouse who is instantly ready for sex, while the other spouse needs time to warm up to the idea. In other words, one of you is a microwave and the other one is a Crock-Pot®. Scheduling sex is like turning on the Crock-Pot®. So schedule it.

After I spoke on this topic at an event, one couple wrote to me and said: "We have officially determined that Saturday is sex day. It's kind of a joke, but we hardly ever miss a Saturday. This helps us to go ahead and start heating up the Crock-Pot®."

What does that look like in the real world?

Sex
Now it's your turn:
Who: _____
What: _____
When: _____
Where: _____
How: _____

Fun is not always easy, but it is always necessary for a great marriage.

There was a season in my life when I didn't live that out. I consider myself a pretty fun guy. In fact, it's a good thing I'm fun. I'm pretty sure my wife wouldn't have chosen me solely based on my level of eye-candy-ness. However, we had a season of our life that was anything but fun.

My mom passed away when I was 10. Her sister, who was only 12 years older than me, stepped in and helped raise my brother and me. I loved my aunt; oh, how I loved her. Then, tragedy struck again: Her son, who was like my brother, passed away suddenly at age 25. Two years later, my aunt passed away suddenly at age 49.

I was rocked. I was numb. I was no fun. Sure, I faked it with my kids with limited success. But there was no faking it with my wife. She knew I was hurt, and she was amazing at letting me grieve.

But my grief made me distant. My grief made me serious. Don't get me wrong—I helped create some moments of awesome, but for the most part I wasn't 100 percent for several . . . gulp . . . years.

One day I realized how serious I had become when I said something truly witty, truly funny, and my wife responded back with a serious look and some "mmmhhh" to illustrate she felt my pain.

I actually said to her, "Wait, why are you mmmhhhing me? That was funny."

The look on her face was priceless and cautiously optimistic when she said, "That was supposed to be funny?" She was hopeful that I was coming back to her. And I was.

When I started to come out of what I now call "the funk," I was ready to have fun again. In fact, I made a decision to put my grief behind me because, as cliché as it may sound, that is what my aunt would have wanted. I made a decision to be fun again. While I was a little rusty, my old favorites still worked. I busted out my classic fun move: Walk in the room not saying anything while wearing my scuba skins. I chose fun movies and music instead of sad movies and music. I made a point to laugh. I listened and watched for humor; I found it and lightened up. Nancie was so glad that fun Ted was back.

I regret not bouncing back sooner. I regret that I didn't laugh more. I regret I didn't cling to Proverbs 17:22:

> *A cheerful heart is good medicine, but a*
> *crushed spirit dries up the bones*
> *(NIV).*

Had my aunt had the opportunity, I'm pretty sure she would have come down and kicked my butt for being so serious and sad, and she would have told me to get back to fully loving my wife and kids.

Yes, life is serious. But we don't always have to be. Be fun, because it connects your US in a way nothing else can. Fun is the get-to of our lives that keeps the have-tos more in perspective. So be fun. Make time for fun. Make it a habit to **Have Serious Fun**.

You can do it. It's essential to your US.

Wait. Did I just close out a chapter on fun with a story about two tragic deaths? I think I did. Probably shouldn't have done that. So I will close with this:

Why did the cow cross the road? To get to the udder side.*

Now, that feels better.

(*Joke courtesy of my daughter, Teddie Lowe.)

CHAPTER 4

Your Best Us

Love God First

When I talk to couples in conflict, most of them—no, all of them—tend to do this: They want to give me all the details about the issues they are having in their US.

She will say that he spent $30 more on fishing equipment than they had agreed to spend. He will say that he made that $30 back by providing dinner with the fish he caught.

He will say she was 45 minutes late getting home from work because of a budget meeting. She will say she was only 32 minutes late, and it wasn't a budget meeting—it was a contract meeting.

She will say he agreed to paint the garage before summer. He will say he said no such thing.

In the same way, when I talk to couples who have turned their marriages around, they also want to give me all the details of the things they are now doing to make their marriages work.

He will say they have started spending a lot of time together. She will say they have learned how to better communicate.

He will say the sex is better than ever. She will say she's glad he thinks the sex is better than ever.

Regardless of whether married people are sharing the bad or the good with me, they seem to think their marriages depend solely on their relationships with each other. This is a logical thought because this is true for most of us. The condition of our marriage tends to go up or down depending on how well we are managing our marriage. No matter where our marriage is on the marital yo-yo continuum, most of us maintain a level of hope that we could be more of what we want to be.

Why? For some of us, it's simple. At some point our US was working, and we think maybe, just maybe, we can get ourselves back there. For some of us, our US has never felt like it was working, and we think maybe if we just do the right things, then it would get better. We hope things will change when (fill-in-the-blank) changes, i.e., when the kids move out, when work slows down, when we learn how to communicate.

We think reading a book, this book, might just be the thing that helps us to behave our way to a better US. Most married people still have . . . if even just a little . . . hope.

But on the flip side of hope is worry. We worry that our US will never be what we want it to be. We worry that we won't be able to do all the things or be all the things we should be. All too often, we do things we don't want to do, and we don't do things we want to do. In ordinary situations, this mismanagement of our marriage can show up in ways that cause damage to our US.

- You arrive home exhausted from work. Your spouse wants to share their day with you. You dissolve into the sofa instead.

- You are frustrated that your spouse has left their towel on the floor for the millionth time, and you let them know it in a cutting, sarcastic way.
- Your spouse can't understand how you are okay relaxing on a Saturday when the garage is a mess. So you "clean" the garage by slamming everything into place.
- Your spouse says something that hurts your feelings. Instead of addressing it, you shut them out for days.

Why do we do these sorts of things? Maybe the more important question is, why can't we simply do better?
Maybe we are not sure how to "do better."
Maybe it's because we simply don't try to "do better."
Maybe we are tired of trying to "do better."
Maybe it's because our spouse isn't trying to "do better."

Whatever the reason, we can find ourselves stuck in an US where no one is happy.

So what do we do?
Some of us try harder.
Some of us stop trying but stay together for the kids.
Some of us stop trying but stay together because we don't believe in divorce.
Some of us stop trying altogether. We separate or divorce.

We think the answers to our marriage lie solely within our marriage. We believe the answers lie in unraveling the mystery of our marriage or by doing better or being better. While obviously the dynamics between the two of you are important, and those dynamics make up much of the focus of this book, there is another relationship that I think matters even more—your individual relationship with God.

As soon as you read that last sentence, I know that you might have been tempted to toss the book aside or skip to the next chapter for several reasons. Because, for one, you feel like you've heard this part before: "Yeah, yeah, pray together, do devotions together, etc., etc."

Two, you are not sure how you feel about the whole God thing.

Three, you aren't where you want to be with God, and because of that, you think God won't do that "thing" to help your marriage, whatever that "thing" is.

I get it. Oh, how I get it.
At one point in my life, I was an example of one, two, and three.

But please hang in there for the next few pages. I think you will find something a little unexpected and a lot relevant, no matter where you are with God. I think you will be encouraged regardless of where you are in your faith. Why? Because this habit, **Love God First**, has the potential to make your US something that surprises you. In fact, I believe Love God First is the most important habit in this book.

So why am I talking about the habit of Love God First after the habit of Have Serious Fun? Because I have found that it is fun that frequently opens our heart to better understand that God is crazy about us.

The habit to Love God First begins with a question for Jesus. With the goal of discrediting Him, a group of religious leaders, known as the Pharisees, asked Jesus a question. This account is found in Mark 12:28–31:

> *One of the teachers of the law came and heard them debating. Noticing that Jesus had given them a good answer, he asked him, "Of all the commandments, which is the most important?"*
> *"The most important one," answered Jesus, "is this: 'Hear, O Israel: The Lord our God, the Lord is one. Love the Lord your God with all your heart and with all your soul and with all your mind and with all your strength.' The second is this: 'Love your neighbor as yourself.' There is no commandment greater than these" (NIV).*

We could talk forever about the power of these verses in your marriage. But I want to make one simple but powerful observation: Notice in these verses the order in which Jesus commands us to love. As much as He wants us to love people, He wants us to love Him first. Because when our connection with God is growing, it postures us to love others better than we could ever love them on our own. **Something changes inside of us that radically impacts the things that come out of us.**

Quite simply, connection with God makes us better spouses. Things come out of us that can even surprise us. Things come of us that can really surprise our spouse. And these things describe the spouse most of us want to be. What are these things? Galatians 5:22–23 (NIV) contains a list of the fruit we bear in our lives when we Love God First. These are called the fruit of the Spirit:

Something changes inside of us that radically impacts the things that come out of us.

> love,
> joy,
> peace,
> forbearance (patience),
> kindness,
> goodness,
> faithfulness,
> gentleness, and
> self-control.

While these words describe a great spouse, chances are this list may frustrate or discourage you because these characteristics don't describe you, at least not all of them. If you are thinking, "I can never be all these things," you would be correct. You can't. That's the whole point.

While you may sometimes have a little bit of patience with your spouse, God constantly has enormous patience with you.

While you can only extend kindness to your spouse for so long, God is eternally kind to you.

While you can lose self-control with your spouse, God is in total control of how He loves you.

When we connect to God, we become more like God, and that flows out of us onto our spouse. What do I mean by connecting with God? I will get to that in a minute. For now, consider this: What's flowing out of you? Today? Yesterday? What do you want to flow out of you?

Love or apathy?
Joy or sorrow?
Peace or insecurity?
Patience or impatience?
Kindness or unkindness?
Goodness or badness?
Faithfulness or unfaithfulness?
Gentleness or harshness?
Self-control or recklessness?

My friend Jeff Henderson asks the question this way:

"What is like to be on the other side of me?"

That's a powerful, yet often convicting question. But the great news is that God wants to help you be a better you. Marriages that work do so because both spouses tend to be loving, joyful, peaceful, patient, kind, good, faithful, gentle and self-controlled. Non-Christians can exemplify these things as well. But when we are connected to the One who is the source of those things, we can love in a way we could never love on our own and beyond our own limits.

But I tend to complicate the simplicity of this truth, trying to make things happen on my own and making a mess of the situation. It helps me when I go back to the basics of my faith.

God wants to help you be a better you.

When I decided to follow Jesus as a child, a pastor explained that because of that decision, I had received a gift. A gift? He said I had the power of the Holy Spirit living inside of me. When you tell an imaginative seven-year-old he has a ghost living inside of him, that can be tricky. Reading my reaction, the pastor said, "Don't think of it as a ghost, but as a Spirit." He said, "God's powerful Spirit is living in you. And you can ask Him to help you. He is right there always inside of you." (See 2 Corinthians 5:5.) I have found the pastor's words to be true ever since.

Don't get me wrong; there were huge seasons of my life when I tried to block and tackle the Holy Spirit. Even now, I can tune Him out in a New York minute. But when I slow down, breathe, and say to God, "Help me to be the man, the husband You want me to be," He changes me. He changes our US, because in those moments I trust Him. He meets needs only He can meet. And I stop trying to get too much from Nancie.

Yes, God can use Nancie to make me feel accepted, loved, secure, and valued. But to expect 100% of *all that* from Nancie is not only unfair, it's impossible. Yes, she is amazing, but she isn't God, and she isn't just my wife. Nancie is also a mom of three, daughter of two, sister of two, friend of many, employee of a company, volunteer in a school, and more. There is only so much she can give.

In her book *Hold Me Tight*, Dr. Sue Johnson states it this way:

> "Most of us no longer live in supportive communities with our birth families and childhood friends close at hand. We work longer and longer hours, commute further and further distances, and thus have fewer and fewer opportunities to develop close relationships. Most often, the couples I see in my practice live in a community of two . . . . Inevitably, we now ask our lovers for the emotional connection and sense of belonging that my grandmother got from a village."[8]

That's simply too much pressure for any spouse.

What if we removed the extreme pressure we put on our spouse to meet our huge emotional and relational needs? (I can almost hear the collective sigh of relief from our spouses.) What would happen? Amazing things for certain. And we remove that pressure by connecting with God and allowing Him to meet our deepest needs.

So, finally, what do I mean by *connecting* with God?

Throughout this book you will hear me encouraging you that your US is unique, and what works for your US may not work for others. There is no other US like yours. This is true, in part, because there is no one else on the earth just like you. God created you to be you. So how you connect with God may be different from the way I connect with God.

What if we removed the extreme pressure we put on our spouse to meet our huge emotional and relational needs?

For me, I connect with God by typing my prayers into a document in my computer. I have done that consistently for years. Before I start typing my prayers, I get down on my knees and tell God He is King and I am not. Then I read a passage of Scripture or a devotional. Then, as I am writing my prayers, I use the acronym C.H.A.T, which stands for Confess, Honor, Ask, and Thank. While that may sound a little cheesy, it really helps me connect with God. But don't get me wrong, my prayers don't read like beautiful poetry. In fact, I recently read back through several months of my prayers. In the name of full disclosure, some of it seemed like the ramblings of a crazy person. But it works for me. How do I know? Because I tend to be more loving, joyful, peaceful, patient, kind, good, faithful, gentle, and self-controlled on the days I take time to connect with God. I'm not perfect, but I am more of those things on the days I connect and stay connected to God.

Writing my prayers to God connects me with God, which makes me a better husband. That's what works for me. But typing your prayers may not work for you. It doesn't work for Nancie; Nancie prays when she runs. So many of our conversations start with her saying, "Today when I was praying on my run, I thought . . . " She then goes on to describe how her perspective became clearer, more forgiving, more peaceful.

One of my best friends says he gets closer to God on his motorcycle. While my past experiences with motorcycles have made me a little paranoid to drive a one, it works for him. For others, getting close to God comes during times of worship through music. For others, getting close to God comes through acts of service.

So how about you? What makes you closer to God? Maybe you don't know yet. Maybe you don't have a clue. That's okay. God is much more patient than we are.

When I was praying for the action step for this chapter about loving God first, I struggled because everything I landed on seemed too limiting of God and of you. While the C.H.A.T. acronym works for me, I certainly don't want it to serve as anything more than an example. More than anything formulaic, at the end of this chapter, I want to encourage you to make one move toward connecting more with God. At the same time, I do want to give you something to help you make loving God first a habit.

MAKE IT A HABIT

LOVE GOD FIRST

Choose from the list on the next page or come up with your own way of connecting with God, and practice that habit for seven days.

- Don't know how you feel about God? Tell Him that on the way to work, and ask Him to help you love your spouse more.
- Read one chapter a day from the book of Proverbs for 31 days.
- Join a small group or class at church.
- Talk to God in the morning.
- Talk to God at night.
- Invite Him into the tough moments when you are having tension with your spouse. Pray, "God, help me to know how to love in this situation."
- Pray before you reconnect with your spouse at the end of the day.
- Say a prayer for your spouse before talking about something that is bothering you.
- Read two Bible verses in the morning. Read two at lunch. Read two at night.

So go tell your spouse you need a motorcycle to connect to God. Whatever you decide, whatever works for you, can I encourage you to do one thing more to connect with Him in a way that works for you?

Bottom line: Find your way to talk to God and read His words, the Bible. When we do those two things, God lets us know Him. We learn how to love Him. We learn how to love others.

Part of the heart of this chapter is to help you find God the easy way. Because I'm the guy that often learns the hard way. But God is gracious with me. In fact, there is one argument in our marriage that God used to help me find Him. In this argument, I was going through the list of things I felt Nancie was doing wrong. I will never forget the moment when she screamed, "What do you want me to do!?" I was shocked because I had absolutely no answer to her question. I didn't know what I wanted her to do. For good reason, she couldn't do anything to fix what was broken inside of me. The problem wasn't with her.

Not long after this fight, I sought wisdom from a man who wasn't perfect but who had a great relationship with God and with his wife. While this friend helped me work through some really difficult things from my childhood, the greatest thing he did was encourage me to simply talk to God.

So after I would meet with him, I would talk to God in my car on the way to work. I'm sure people around me thought I was crazy, but I was at a point where I didn't care. As I simply talked more with God, I became more of who I *wanted* to be and more of who Nancie *needed* me to be. Me connecting more with God changed me. It changed our US. How? It's hard for me to explain, because it's beautiful and mysterious and unique to our US, but I think these words from the movie *Shadowlands*[9], depicting the life of author C.S. Lewis, come pretty close:

> "I pray because I can't help myself. I pray because I'm helpless. I pray because the need flows out of me all the time, waking and sleeping. It doesn't change God; it changes me."

It changes me too. I pray the same for you.

CHAPTER

Your Best Us

Respect and Love

My wife and I would say we have been enjoying our US for many years. That's largely because we try to do the things I'm encouraging all of us to do in this book. I can say with all integrity that we've made these things habits in our lives.

But recently, our US went sideways. Our US got ugly. I was having a "discussion" with our 15-year-old when Nancie entered the room. She quickly joined the conversation and I felt—notice I said, "*I felt*"—like she was siding with our son, and against me.

I was then not only frustrated with my son, I was also mad at my wife. I "ended" the argument by leaving the room, saying some things on the way out that I would soon regret. I then decided that not only was I going to leave the room, I was going to leave the house altogether. As I drove away, I immediately started telling myself all the things I "deserved" to hear: "How could she not support me? I'm a great dad (most of the time.) I needed her and she took his side. She made me look like an idiot."

I was mentally and emotionally justifying the terrible way I responded. In my lingering anger, I even canceled the small group meeting we were having at our house that night.

A few hours later, I came back to reality, asking myself what had happened. How could I just flip out like that? I know better. Yes, I responded like that earlier in our marriage, but I hadn't done that in a really long time. So why start back now?

I greatly regretted and still regret the argument. I apologized to both Nancie and our son, and they have both forgiven me. We have moved on. But I know that I created a moment that will unfortunately linger, at least to some degree, for a really long time.

Maybe you relate. Your button gets pushed and you react in a way that you later wish you hadn't. Maybe you get sarcastic. You pout. You refuse to talk about it. You get loud. You get needy. But why do we get so worked up? Why do we have stupid fights about stupid things? Why do we let stupid fights damage our US?

Why? For starters, every behavior has a payoff, even when we respond in a way that hurts our marriage. Take anger, for instance. There are several immediate payoffs to anger:
We get our spouse's attention.
It feels pretty great to release our tension and stress.
We get revenge.

There is even a chemical payoff to anger. No one is yawning when they are angry. Studies show that when we are angry, neurotransmitter chemicals are released into the brain and body that give us a jolt of energy[10]. These findings are fascinating to me. But then again, I geek out about this sort of stuff. While I love brain chemical studies, I love what we are about to look at much more.

Here's where it all started. In the spring of 2004, I was meeting with a counselor and we were talking about better ways for me to respond to Nancie during conflict. When this topic came up during our session, I thought I knew what was coming. I was pretty sure he was going to teach me the newest communication skill.

Instead, he asked me a seemingly simple question. He said, "What is the thing about Nancie that drives you the craziest?" I didn't have to think about it for long. I said, "I feel like when I ask her to help me do something, she acts selfishly." I went on to give him examples. He said, "Tonight, I want you to ask Nancie what it is about *you* that drives her the craziest."

Then he said something that would become incredibly eye-opening for me, and hopefully for you. He said, "I bet the thing about her that drives you the craziest and the thing about you that drives her the craziest are chasing each other."

I didn't wait until that night. I called Nancie from the parking lot of the counselor's office. After assuring her I really did want her to answer honestly, I asked, "What is the thing I do that drives you the craziest?" Without a second of delay she said, "When you ask me to do something for you, I think you are being manipulative."

There it was. Because I didn't want her to do that *thing* she does when I ask her to help me, I would dance around the request like a landmine. The way I asked for help went a little something like this:

"Hey, if you have time today—but if you don't have time today, don't worry about it—but if you do happen to have time in the midst of your crazy day, can you please pick up my computer? I thought you might have time because the computer store is close to Wal-Mart, and I know you are going there today. But if you don't have time, don't worry about it. But if you do have time, that would be great. But if you don't, don't worry about it."

For some reason that frustrated her. I can't imagine why! But I read her frustrations as selfishness. I responded to her frustrations by getting defensive, telling her I couldn't believe she was bothered by such a simple request especially since I told her she didn't have to . . . blah, blah, blah. At that end of my blah, blah, blahs, or maybe before, she would shut down, get quiet, and become short with her answers. And the more she shut down, the more I tried to defend myself—and the more I tried to defend myself, the more she shut down. And around and around we would go.

My counselor was right. These two *things* were chasing each other. This was very helpful for our marriage. Now when I need a favor from her, I ask her differently. Now I simply call and say, "Pick up my computer, jerk!" It's become our joke. She laughs and tells me if she can or can't. Just knowing what was really going on between us during these times of tension turned one of our biggest sources of conflict into a fun banter.

While understanding that our negative responses were chasing each other was so powerful, I wanted to go even deeper. I wanted to find out what else we didn't know—not just for us, but also for the couples I worked with.

Specifically, I wanted to know **why** we were responding that way. I understood how our negative responses triggered each other, but why were we so touchy in these areas? What was beneath our responses? What I discovered has been revolutionary for our US and so many others.

Let's start with a big picture view.

During times of conflict, why do so many of us respond in a way that hurts our US?

Quite simply, we are imperfect people born to imperfect people. We all come into this world a little, if not a lot broken. If you need evidence, go spend five minutes with a toddler, or sit for five minutes in bumper-to-bumper traffic. We all have our junk. As a Christian I believe we are born with a sin nature.

We are broken. And we bring this brokenness into our marriage. Our brokenness married our spouse's brokenness. And marriage has a way of revealing our brokenness. But because we are so familiar with our own brokenness, it is easy to only see our spouse's brokenness.

An air freshener company markets their product by illustrating how we can become "nose-blind" to our homes and cars. One example of this is a teenager's room that smells fine to the teenager, but his mom thinks it smells like a high school locker room. (That kid lives at my house, by the way.) In the same way, we get blind to our own brokenness. And then we get married and all we know is that before we got married, we didn't do that *thing* we do during conflict, at least not as much. Before we got married, we didn't get so frustrated. We didn't get so angry. We didn't get so hurt. We didn't get so defensive. We didn't shut down so quickly.

So we do the logical, relational math: If I didn't act this way before we got married, then the problem must be my spouse.

You often hear people say, "He/she just brings out the worst in me!" Our spouse doesn't bring out the worse in us; they reveal the brokenness in us. In the same way, marriage brings out our spouse's brokenness. And they, like us, can often notice our brokenness more than their own.

The combination of your brokenness and your spouse's brokenness can equal many things. For you, maybe the combination of your brokenness is a relational speed bump that you would avoid if you knew how. Or maybe the combination of your brokenness hurts your US on a regular basis. Or maybe the combination of your brokenness has led you to believe that divorce is your only option.

Now let's zoom in a little closer.

> # Our spouse doesn't bring out the worse in us; they reveal the brokenness in us.

We all came into marriage with varying levels of hurt from significant people in our lives. The sum total of the hurt from our parent(s) or other significant people in our lives can send messages that are seared into the very core of who we are. The messages are lies. Let me say it again because this is key: These hurtful messages are lies. And I'm not talking about your behavior; your behavior may be bad. I'm talking about someone telling you that in one way or another that you are no good. But this is a lie because God doesn't make junk.

Ladies, maybe your mom or a group of girls made comments about your weight when you were growing up, and the lie that you are not beautiful is written on your heart. I worked in youth ministry for years and I was always amazed at how girls could remember verbatim what someone had said about them, especially if it was something about their appearance.

One of the young ladies we worked with told Nancie and I that she was really struggling because she was so overweight and unattractive. This was absolutely not the case. But as she unpacked past comments from her dad and siblings, it made sense. These comments had written a lie on her heart, a lie that she believed much more than the mirror! We tried to reassure her that their comments were not true, but she dismissed it as us "just being nice." What led her to believe this? Words.

Hurtful words from broken people write lies on our hearts.

Perhaps there is no greater evidence that we are broken than the words that come out of our mouths. Since the beginning of time, it appears that words matter and are a huge part of our relational DNA.

Proverbs 12:18 says:

Careless words stab like a sword, but wise words bring healing (NCV).

Careless words can be like a stabbing. And a stabbing is an event that if it happened to you or to me, we would never forget. Yes, words can be a stabbing that we remember. Careless, hurtful words from broken people write lies on our hearts. People write lies on our hearts. The great news is that we don't have to live in a cycle of hurting each other. We can live in a marriage that gets into a cycle of respect and love—which you're about to unpack, as you discover how to . . .

MAKE IT A
HABIT

RESPECT AND LOVE

Let's take a look at our day-to-day interaction as an US. This is where things can get really clear. This is where your understanding can start to heal your brokenness.

I'm going to walk you through two exercises designed to reveal what you are really fighting about. Now, I know the word exercises makes most of us want to run, and not in the healthy way. But I promise they are worth it. PROMISE.

Ideally it's best if you go through this process with your spouse, but if your spouse isn't interested, what you are going to learn about yourself can still be huge for you and your marriage. Why? Because it always takes two to keep a negative chase going, but often it just takes one to stop it.

The Negative Chase

I will never forget that line from my counselor: "Those two things are chasing each other." Our organization, MarriedPeople, has expanded this idea to help you understand not only what is chasing what during your conflicts, but also why there is a negative chase to begin with. We have also added the Positive Chase exercise to help you learn a better way. And when chasing is positive, it's a good, good thing.

Before I walk you step by step through this process, I am going to unpack the Negative Chase in our marriage, which will hopefully make understanding your own Negative Chase easier.

For Nancie and I to understand our Negative Chase we had to discover four things:

1. Ted's negative response,

2. The lie written on Ted's heart,

3. Nancie's negative response, and

4. The lie written on Nancie's heart.

Let's go back to the tension I wrote about at the beginning of this chapter.

When I felt like Nancie was taking our 15-year-old's side, my negative response was to get defensive. This conflict connected to the lie written on my heart that I'm inadequate.
Growing up, I was told daily that something was wrong with me. I believed it. Even after seeing a counselor off and on for many years and being a naturally introspective person, there are moments when I still feel inadequate.

The conflict I was having with my son was making me feel like I was inadequate as a dad. I was truly trying to help my son, but he wasn't allowing it because he is, well, a teenager.

When Nancie stepped in and told me to calm down and listen to him, I didn't. In that moment, the lie that I am inadequate was screaming at me. I defended myself instead of doing what I needed to do: love and care for my son and wife.

So what did I do when I felt inadequate in this situation? My negative response was to get defensive.

One defensive thing I said to Nancie was, "You didn't have my back. I needed you to be on my team." My defensiveness tapped the lie written on her heart, which is that she doesn't measure up.

Who wrote that lie on her heart? Her mom? No. Her dad? No. As she was growing up, she knew that she measured up. She excelled at almost everything she tried. In fact, she was high school valedictorian, head cheerleader, and received a full college scholarship. So who wrote the lie on her heart that she didn't measure up? Gulp . . . me. So why did I write that lie on her heart?

As I have mentioned earlier, marriage reveals our brokenness. It surely did in me. There was a season early in our marriage when I was feeling terrible much of the time; I was depressed, anxious, and feeling inadequate at my job. I thought some of this "terrible" had to be caused by Nancie. So when we would argue, I would get defensive and list all the ways she wasn't doing what she should do and all the ways I was doing what I should do. The sum total of my negative response when we argued, wrote a lie on her heart that she didn't measure up.

I wrote that lie on my precious wife's heart. But now I work really hard to never communicate that she doesn't measure up. However, on the day we had the big argument about our son, I regressed back to my defensiveness, leading her to believe the lie that she did not measure up.

When I did that, she got angry and shut down, which tapped that lie on my heart that I'm inadequate, and I responded by getting defensive, which tapped the lie on her heart that she doesn't measure up, at which point she shut down, and around and around we go in our Negative Chase we go. See the next page.

NEGATIVE CHASE

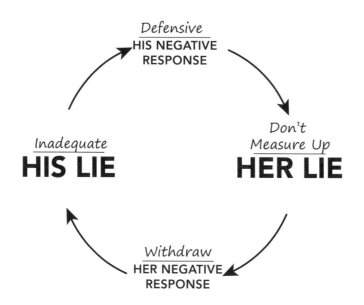

Now it's your turn. And while it may be uncomfortable to dig up the past and discover things about yourself and your spouse that are hard to see, I promise you will be glad you did. Promise.

If you're like me, you tend to skip things like this. Please don't. It's worth it.

To understand your negative chase as a couple, you need to discover four things that happened in your past conflict(s):

1. Your negative response,

2. The lie written on your heart,

3. Your spouse's negative response, and

4. The lie written on your spouse's heart.

Let's dive in.

Negative Chase Step 1: Your Negative Response

Think about your latest conflict. It doesn't have to be anything "important," just whatever it was that caused friction. **What was your negative response?** Below are common responses during times of conflict.

✓ Put a check by all the words that describe your typical response during conflict.
★ Put a star by the one that seems to be the most accurate.

Once you have narrowed it down to the word that best describes your typical response, insert your negative response into the Negative Chase exercise on page 71.

Withdrawal	Complaining/criticism
Escalation	Striking out
Earn-it mode	Manipulation
Negative beliefs	Anger or rage
Blaming	Catastrophizing
Exaggeration	Emotional shut-down
Tantrums	Humor
Denial	Sarcasm
Invalidation	Minimization
Defensiveness	Rationalization
Clinginess	Indifference
Passive-aggression	Abdication
Caretaking	Self-abandonment
Acting out	Other
Fix-it mode	

[If you would like further definitions of any of these feeling-oriented words, see Appendix A.]

Negative Chase Step 2: Lie Written on Your Heart

Conflict reveals the lie written on your heart through past relationships or your current relationship with each other. You discover that lie by asking yourself: **How did that conflict make me think and feel about myself?**

Below are some words to choose from that define the lie written on your heart.

✔ Put a check by all the words that relate to what you felt during that conflict.

★ Put a star by the one that seems to be the most accurate.

Rejected	Dissatisfied
Abandoned	Cheated
Disconnected	Worthless/devalued
Like a failure	Unaccepted
Helpless/powerless	Judged
Defective	Humiliated
Inadequate	Ignored
Inferior	Unimportant
Invalidated	Other
Unloved	

[If you would like further definitions of any of these feeling-oriented words, see Appendix B.]

Negative Chase Step 3: Complete the Negative Chase

Once you and your spouse have finished Steps 1 and 2, exchange answers and insert your spouse's negative response and the lie written on your spouse's heart into the Negative Chase diagram below.

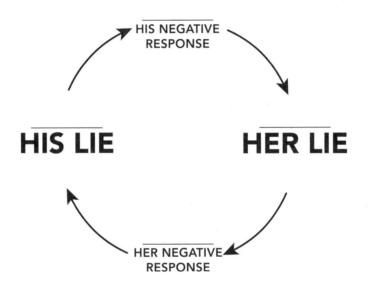

You may be thinking like so many couples before you, now that we understand our Negative Chase, what can we do about it? The next step is to discover and start to live out a different kind of chase, a Positive Chase.

As I did with the Negative Chase, I will unpack the Positive Chase in our marriage to hopefully help you understand your Positive Chase more clearly.

POSITIVE CHASE

For Nancie and I to understand our Positive Chase, we had to discover four things:

1. Ted's positive response,

2. The truth about Ted,

3. Nancie's positive response,

4. The truth about Nancie.

While no change in marriage is instant, changing your Negative Chase is pretty close. Soon after understanding our Negative Chase, I had an opportunity to choose something better.

We were at my parents' home for Christmas, and Nancie was sitting in a chair in the corner of the family room reading a book. I thought, "What is she doing? We don't see my family that often. She should be socializing. It's Christmas. Be with people. Celebrate the birth of Jesus!" I was tempted to say something, but then I stopped and thought. I remembered to look at the situation through the grid of the Positive Chase.

The lie on Nancie's heart: "I don't measure up."

I thought, "Wait a minute. It is fine she is reading a book. My family loves her, and they know she loves them. Relax. Does she measure up to my family? Of course. She serves everyone around her. She cares about every detail of their lives. She spent countless hours buying Christmas presents. Earlier today she was having great conversations with members of my family, and I'm sure she will again later today. And if she doesn't? Everyone will be okay. She deserves a break."

The truth is that Nancie is a child of God. Nancie does measure up. As a Christian, I believe Nancie is God's daughter. How should I treat God's daughter? At least as well as I treat myself! Here is what is true about Nancie. As we have worked out our Positive Chase, Nancie landed on this verse:

> *You have not received a spirit that makes you fearful slaves. Instead, you received God's Spirit when he adopted you as his own children. Now we call him, "Abba, Father" (Romans 8:15 NLT).*

Even when I'm not at my best, Nancie can bank on the truth that she is a child of God, which allows her and even motivates her to stay connected to me, even when she may want to shut down.

Her positive response: stay connected.

When she stays connected to me even when I've responded poorly, it prevents me from feeling inadequate. I can more easily tap into my truth that I'm not inadequate, that *I am fearfully and wonderfully made* (Psalm 139:14 NIV). And when I lean into this truth, it motivates me to change my response from defensive to non-defensive.

My positive response: non-defensive.

When I saw her sitting there reading a book that Christmas, I thought, "I can choose to say something to her about this. After all, it's not healthy to bottle everything up; we need to communicate about things that bother us. BUT . . . is this really the hill I want to die on? If it is, then fine. But just know, you will be telling her once again that she doesn't measure up. So leave her alone. No one cares that she is reading a book."

Conflict avoided. Her lie was not made to feel true. Our US remained intact. See the cycle on the next page.

POSITIVE CHASE

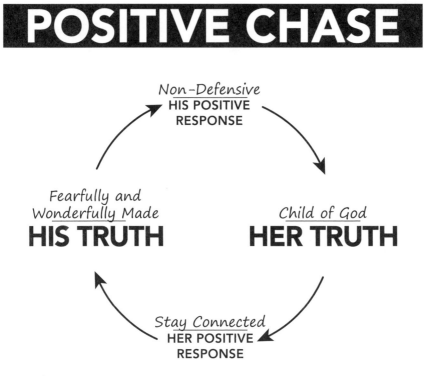

Now it's your turn.

In order to understand your positive chase, you need to discover four things.

1. The truth about you.

2. Your positive response to the truth.

3. The truth about your spouse.

4. Your spouse's positive response to the truth.

Positive Chase Step 1: The Truth about You

On the next pages are some verses from the Bible that speak to what is true about you. Scripture tells us over and over that we are not inadequate and we do measure up, because we are God's children. It is so powerful when we mentally and emotionally swap the lie in our hearts with the truth of who and Whose we are.

Choose from one of the passages below or find a passage on your own that speaks what's REALLY true about you.

✔ Put a check by all the verses that apply.
★ Put a star by the one that applies the most.

Once you have narrowed it down to the verse that best addresses your feelings, insert that truth into the Positive Chase diagram provided on page 79.

If you feel . . .

Rejected
The LORD your God is with you, the Mighty Warrior who saves. He will take great delight in you; in his love he will no longer rebuke you, but will rejoice over you with singing (Zephaniah 3:17 NIV).

Abandoned
The LORD your God is a merciful God; he will not abandon or destroy you or forget the covenant with your ancestors, which he confirmed to them by oath (Deuteronomy 4:31 NIV).

Disconnected
Be strong and courageous. Do not be afraid or terrified because of them, for the LORD your God goes with you; he will never leave you nor forsake you (Deuteronomy 31:6 NIV).

Like a Failure
"For I know the plans I have for you," declares the LORD, "plans to prosper you and not to harm you, plans to give you hope and a future" (Jeremiah 29:11 NIV).

Helpless/Powerless

I can do all this through him who gives me strength (Philippians 4:13 NIV).

Defective

I praise you because I am fearfully and wonderfully made; your works are wonderful, I know that full well (Psalm 139:14 NIV).

Inadequate

There are different kinds of gifts, but the same Spirit distributes them (1 Corinthians 12:4 NIV).

Inferior

"For God so loved the world that he gave his one and only Son, that whoever believes in him shall not perish but have eternal life" (John 3:16 NIV).

Invalidated

He who did not spare his own Son, but gave him up for us all—how will he not also, along with him, graciously give us all things? (Romans 8:32 NIV).

Unloved

See what great love the Father has lavished on us, that we should be called children of God! And that is what we are! (1 John 3:1).

Dissatisfied

Godliness with contentment is great gain (1 Timothy 6:6 NIV).

Cheated

The Lord is not slow in keeping his promise, as some understand slowness. Instead he is patient with you, not wanting anyone to perish, but everyone to come to repentance (2 Peter 3:9 NIV).

Worthless/Devalued

But God demonstrates his own love for us in this: While we were still sinners, Christ died for us (Romans 5:8).

Unaccepted

"I will ask the Father, and he will give you another advocate to help you and be with you forever" (John 14:16 NIV).

Judged

Therefore, there is now no condemnation for those who are in Christ Jesus (Romans 8:1 NIV)

Humiliated

Let us then with confidence draw near to the throw of grace, that we may receive mercy and find grace to hope in time of need. (Hebrews 4:16 NIV)

Ignored

Indeed, the very hair of your head are all numbered. Don't be afraid; you are worth more than many sparrows (Luke 12:7 NIV)

Unimportant

Through him all things were made; without him nothing was made that has been made (John 1:3 NIV)

Positive Chase Step 2: Your Response to the Truth

Based on the truth, you can choose a different response. Choose your own positive response, or choose from this list. Write your response and the truth in the diagram provided on page 79.

✔ Put a check by 1–4 ways that you can act if you are living in the truth.
★ Put a star by the one that you think will honor your spouse the most.

Accepting	Settled
Nurturing	Seeking good
Supportive	Merciful
Encouraging	Loving
Giving	Valuing self
Welcoming	Positive
Kind	Joyful
Gentle	Turning from addictive behaviors
Listening	Energetic
Empathetic	Hopeful
Humble	Respectful
Inclusive	Open
Patient	Intimate
Forgiving	Able to be present
Compassionate	Responsible
Non-defensive	Trustworthy
Vulnerable	Honest
Communicating care	Reliable
Engaging	Connecting with others
Peaceful	Self-controlled
Relaxed	Transparent

Positive Chase Steps 3 & 4: Complete the Positive Chase

Once you and your spouse have finished Steps 1 and 2, exchange answers and insert your spouse's positive response and their truth into the Positive Chase diagram below.

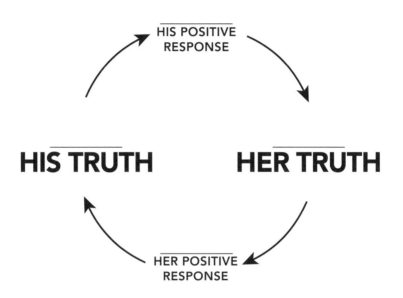

And what happens when you live out the Positive Chase? When we are living out the Positive Chase, we are living out the chase described in Ephesians 5, the chase of respect and love.

In Ephesians 5:21, Paul writes: *Submit to one another out of reverence for Christ (NIV).*

This Positive Chase begins with mutual respect. What if we simply respected our spouse? Because no matter what word you chose for your positive response, it contains an element of respect.

As you go deeper into Ephesians 5, Paul speaks to husbands and wives separately. He repeats himself, and I'm assuming to make his point.

Wives, submit yourselves to your own husbands as you do to the Lord. For the husband is the head of the wife as Christ is the head of the church, his body, of which he is the Savior. Now as the church submits to Christ, so also wives should submit to their husbands in everything. Husbands, love your wives, just as Christ loved the church and gave himself up for her to make her holy, cleansing her by the washing with water through the word, and to present her to himself as a radiant church, without stain or wrinkle or any other blemish, but holy and blameless. In this same way, husbands ought to love their wives as their own bodies. He who loves his wife loves himself. After all, no one ever hated their own body, but they feed and care for their body, just as Christ does the church—for we are members of his body. "For this reason a man will leave his father and mother and be united to his wife, and the two will become one flesh." This is a profound mystery—but I am talking about Christ and the church. However, each one of you also must love his wife as he loves himself, and the wife must respect her husband (Ephesians 5:22-33 NIV).

So what is required of husbands in this passage? Unconditional love. That's right, guys, we are to love our wives as Christ loves the church. Christ died for the church. So when a man uses this passage to insinuate that God has made him the boss of his wife, it blows my mind. Men, we are to serve our wives, lay down our lives for our wives . . . unconditionally. That's a tall order, a big responsibility. So when our wives are unkind, we are to be kind. When our wives do things that frustrate us, we need to think about how we are thinking. We need to ask ourselves constantly, "Am I unconditionally loving my wife?"

This passage also tells women to respect their husbands, to unconditionally respect their husbands.

Commanding a wife to unconditionally respect her husband, who may or may not deserve her respect, feels so 2,000-years-ago. After all, doesn't respect have to be earned? The command for a wife to unconditionally respect her husband seems to make the wife less-than. But this isn't about hierarchy; it's about heart.

Paul knew then what is still true today: A man craves respect more than anything in the world. So is Paul saying women don't want respect?

Not even remotely. That's why he started with mutual respect in verse 21. Men AND women need respect and love. When both men and women are in the cycle of respect and love, that is the most Positive Chase of them all.

Respect isn't about hierarchy; it's about heart.

Marriage researchers have found the same to be true. In their book *How to Improve Your Marriage Without Talking About It*, authors Dr. Steven Stosny and Pat Love, Ph.D., unpack how couples disconnect due to a cycle of fear and shame.[11] Or to use our words, couples disconnect due to a Negative Chase of fear and shame. For example, while both men and women fear homelessness equally, they do so for different reasons. If you were to ask a woman what she fears about homelessness, she would normally cite harm, isolation, and deprivation. In contrast, most men would say that the most difficult part of being homeless would be feeling like a failure. While safety may be an issue for men, it is the shame of being on the street and unemployed that tends to be their primary concern.

Understanding this difference helps us to keep the connection of our US strong. Men must be conscious not to trigger their wives' fears, and women must be conscious not to shame their husbands. See the cycle on the next page.

CHASE OF FEAR AND SHAME

I find this so compelling because the opposite of respect is shame, and the opposite of love is fear. So when Paul instructs women to respect their husbands and men to unconditionally love their wives, he seems to be tapping into what is innately wired into every man and every woman.

We don't have to do the dance of fear and shame.

There is a different way: We can do the dance, the chase of **respect and love.**

CHAPTER

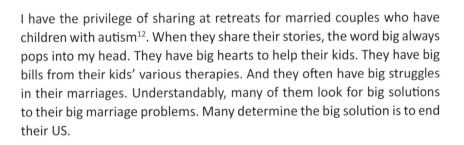

Your Best Us

Practice Your Promise

I have the privilege of sharing at retreats for married couples who have children with autism[12]. When they share their stories, the word big always pops into my head. They have big hearts to help their kids. They have big bills from their kids' various therapies. And they often have big struggles in their marriages. Understandably, many of them look for big solutions to their big marriage problems. Many determine the big solution is to end their US.

Many say things to me like:

- "I just don't have the energy to fight anymore."
- "My relationship with my kid(s) is tough, but I could never leave them. But maybe I *could* leave my spouse."
- "Many people in my situation divorce. No one would blame me."
- "My friends and family would understand that the struggles in my marriage were simply more than I could handle."

After working with these couples, I can see why many of them get to the point where they call it quits. I get it.

But they, like us, promised that forever is forever. While some people write their own vows, most of us promised we would love for richer or for poorer, in sickness and in health, for better or for worse, until death do us part. Either way, all of us made some huge promises, so huge that many of us ask ourselves: Is it really fair to expect anyone to live up to them? Many say no.

Many of us end up saying things like:
"I didn't sign up for this."
"My spouse tricked me."
"It was really great when we were dating, but he turned into a different person once we got married."
"I never dreamed she would have turned into such a workaholic."
"The way we should parent together and the way he parents are light years apart."

Maybe you've had challenges so deep that you have considered or are considering divorce. And here's the hard truth: Depending on the circumstances, maybe you should separate or even divorce. If there is verbal or physical abuse, you need to be apart for a while, and maybe even get divorced. If you or your spouse is a nonrepentant, unremorseful spouse who has cheated or continues to cheat, you need to get out, at least for now and maybe forever. Unfortunately, we have all known people whose only option was divorce.

But after many years of working with couples and examining much research, I can tell you without hesitation: *For most couples, divorce is not the solution to their marital problems.* There are many reasons, but here are just few.

Divorce is not the answer because it often makes everything worse. For example, keeping up two households on the same budget you used to spend on one can be really challenging and, for many, financially devastating.

Divorce is not the answer because your US can be fixed! And it's easier than you may think. In fact, I'm convinced that if most people treated their spouse with the same level of kindness and consideration that they give their coworkers, friends, and even total strangers, their marriages would do a 180. In marriage, many of us give our spouse the worst of us, because we can. If we gave our worst to our jobs, we would be fired. If we gave our worst to our friends, they would find a new friend.

But marriages can be fixed when we change our marital habits. And we CAN change our marital habits. Because we are adults, we can choose how we respond to our spouse in the same way we choose how we treat the other people in our lives. Children only think about what they want in the moment, but adults know that the moment impacts the long-term relationship. We can all love better. We can choose to love better. That's why for most couples, divorce is not the answer.

We can choose to love better.

Divorce is not the answer; **Have Serious Fun is the answer.**
Divorce is not the answer; **Love God First is the answer.**
Divorce is not the answer; **Respect and Love is the answer.**
Divorce is not the answer; **Practice Your Promise is the answer.**
Divorce is not the answer.

Yes, we were all naïve when we got married. No, we didn't know what we had promised. But we promised our spouse's friends and family that they could trust us with their loved-one's life. They trusted us with their beloved son, daughter, sister, brother, friend. We led our future spouse and their family and friends to believe that divorce was not an option. We vowed to be trustworthy. When we live up to that promise, it's a beautiful thing. Research reveals it.

Sociologist Linda Waite from the University of Chicago did a study of 550 adults from a national database. 64% of those who said they were unhappy but stayed together reported they were happy five years later, while 50% of those who divorced or separated felt the same way.

"Permanent marital unhappiness is surprisingly rare," she says.[13]

What? This is so counterintuitive. Don't bad relationships always snowball into really bad relationships? No. Something often happens when a couple goes through challenging times together—their US is more connected than ever on the other side of the challenges.

As I mentioned at the end of chapter three, the sudden deaths of two family members changed me. But instead of Nancie saying, "I didn't sign up for this," she would often just simply pat me on my chest and said, "Oh, your heart. Oh, your broken heart."

While their deaths have left me with a slight but permanent limp, I'm back. I'm fun again. I'm connected with Nancie and the kids. Why? One of the biggest reasons is the way Nancie loved me through it. She loved me because of and in spite of it. Oh, how she practiced what she promised.

When we are there, truly there for our spouse . . .
When we choose to love on days when our spouse's behavior is not lovely, we practice what we promise.
When we choose to love our spouse over loving our need to be right, we practice what we promise.
When we seek help to understand why we are so short-tempered, we practice what we promise.

When we—day by day, situation by situation—practice what we promise, our US can become even more precious than we imagined on the day we said, "I do." It's something beautiful to behold for our kids, our friends, our families, our neighbors, our coworkers, and even strangers.

But how do we do it? How do we faithfully practice what we promised? I believe it rises and falls on a mindset.

As a believer, I follow what Jesus said about staying together forever. Jesus was asked about His mindset concerning divorce. He didn't mince words. If you are a Jesus-follower and struggling in your marriage, these can be pretty tough words to hear.

Once again, with the goal of discrediting Him, a group of religious leaders known as the Pharisees asked Jesus if it is lawful for a man to divorce his wife. Jesus replied:

> *"But at the beginning of creation God 'made them male and female.' 'For this reason a man will leave his father and mother and be united to his wife, and the two will become one flesh.' So they are no longer two, but one flesh. Therefore what God has joined together, let no one separate" (Mark 10:6-9 NIV).*

"Therefore what God has joined together, let no one separate" (Mark 10:9 NIV). No one, including you and including me, should break up our US. In other words, divorce is not an option.

Divorce is not an option? Really? More and more that idea is seen as antiquated, particularly with millennials, 18–34 year olds. Our organization, MarriedPeople, recently put the phrase "Divorce is not an option" out in social media to see what people thought.

One 21-year-old man responded, "Of course divorce is an option. No one should see marriage as a trap."

A 28-year-old woman said, "That's archaic. If someone needs out of marriage, they should have that option."

I understand what they are saying, and to some degree I believe it is true. But again, I daresay that in most cases it is not the right option. People in the counseling community will tell you that as long as divorce is on the table as an option, counselors are very limited with how much they can really help the couple.

Why is this the case? It's an issue of focus. When divorce is on the table as an option, often all people can see is that exit strategy. And I believe that exit strategy is birthed from a mindset. So often people consider divorce because they are running how they view their US through the grid of the **Me Mindset.**

The **Me Mindset** is constantly asking this question: Is this marriage working for me?

It's a big *problem* when we are constantly wondering, "Is this marriage working for me?" Because there are days, weeks, seasons, and perhaps even years when your marriage isn't going to be working for you.

During my time of grief, I'm quite sure my withdrawn, sad demeanor was not working for Nancie. Currently, when I'm frustrated or distant, I'm sure that is not working for her either. When she doesn't stop to spend time with me, that is not working for me.

When your spouse does those things that drive you up the wall, that doesn't work for you. When you do those things that drive your spouse up the wall, that doesn't work for them. To one degree or another, most of us will experience a time when our US is not working for us. The question, "Is this marriage working for me?" can be relationally lethal.

But there is a different question, one that works on the good and the bad days. This is the question that helps us to develop the Core 4 Habit called Practice Your Promise. This question has enormous potential to turn almost any marriage around. And it's a question that reveals the answer to why divorce is usually not the best option.

It's the **Us Mindset.**

The **Us Mindset** asks a better question: What am I doing to make this marriage work?

It's a totally different lens in which to view your marriage. And you are 100-percent responsible for your lens. This is not a question for your spouse; this is a question for you. What am I doing to make this marriage work?

For instance, if you are a spender and your saver spouse is constantly frustrated with you, ask yourself what you are doing to make this marriage work when it comes to money. What can you do? Maybe you have a conversation about how you can talk about money without fighting. Or maybe you simply stop spending so much. At the end of the day, they need to feel like you choose them over things that money can buy. If your spending habits don't work for your spouse, it doesn't work for your US.

If you are an introvert married to an extrovert, social gatherings may never be your thing. Ask yourself, when it comes to being around people, what are you doing to make this marriage work? Maybe you have a conversation with your spouse about what social events they love the most. Then you encourage them to go. Or better yet, you go with them. If people give your spouse energy, you can support them by participating in activities that involve being around people.

Maybe you can't get your spouse to talk to you. Ask yourself, when it comes to communication, what are you doing to make this marriage work? Maybe you take the advice of Steven Stosny and Pat Love from their book *How to Improve Your Marriage Without Talking About It.*[14] Their research found that when a woman asks a man to look into her eyes when they talk, his body floods with a stress-inducing chemical called cortisol, which makes him fidgety and inattentive. It's why men can typically talk more effectively and comfortably when they are driving down the road, raking leaves, or doing something physical.

Making your marriage work means becoming a student of your spouse's strengths and weakness and leveraging both to love them.

One of my many challenges is that I'm terrible with details. I often lose my wallet and my keys, and asking me to do things like make a plane reservation can send me into panic mode. I was ADHD before it was cool, which I know doesn't always work for Nancie. But she loves me by NEVER getting mad at me for losing things. And typically she makes plane reservations for me. That is one of the many things she does to make our marriage work.

Nancie would say one of her challenges is not being able to handle small crowds of people she doesn't really know that well. Recently we had a homeowners association meeting. While Nancie will never lose her keys and can make a plane reservation in a millisecond, she would rather die than to go to that meeting. But I love her. So I went to the meeting. That is one of things that I do to make our marriage work.

While these may be small examples, that's the point. Marriages are made up of micro moves. The sum total of those micro moves equals the condition of your marriage.

Marriages are made up of micro moves. The sum total of those micro moves equals the condition of your marriage.

You may have more power to help your marriage than you think. One of my pet peeves is reading a marriage book where all the applications begin with, "As a couple you need to . . ."

"As a couple you need to pray together." "As a couple you need to do devotionals together." "As a couple you need to budget together."

These are all good things, but couples are almost always at different places when it comes to being proactive or intentional about their marriage. That's why this entire book has been built around helping you help your marriage. If your spouse joins in, fantastic. But you alone can make a huge difference.

As we talked about in chapter five, it always takes two people to keep a negative cycle going, but often it takes only one to stop it. So try to . . .

MAKE IT A HABIT

PRACTICE YOUR PROMISE

For each of the next seven days, view your marriage through the US Mindset:

Today, what am I doing to make this marriage work?

So for example, if you are always fighting about chores, experiment with what happens when you change your approach. If your spouse is messy and you are neat, don't say anything about it or roll your eyes. See what happens. If you are messy and your spouse is neat, be as neat as possible for seven days. See what happens.

You and I get to choose how we act and respond to our spouse, and that is a beautiful thing.
If your spouse loves gifts, buy them one.
If your spouse tends to like sex more often than you, have more sex.
If your spouse loves words of encouragement, write them a note.
If your spouse loves affection, kiss them each day for 30 seconds.
If your spouse wants you to spend time with them, carve out the time.
Whatever speaks love to your spouse, speak it.

When we love our spouse, even when they are irrational, even when their baggage creates an unfair tension, even when they are simply not that lovable, it is powerful for our marriage. It draws them to us.

When we constantly ask ourselves, "What am I doing to make this marriage work?" and then act on the answers to that question, it's a beautiful thing for our US.

Not convinced? Think about this approach in other areas of your life. At work, asking, "What am I doing to make my job work for the company?" can make you an unentitled, happier, and more productive employee.

Or in our friendships, we can ask, "What am I doing to make this friendship work?" The answer to that question could include things like checking on them often, being a great listener, making time for them, being forgiving with them, buying them a gift. We can see why this would draw our friends to us.

But asking what I'm doing to make this marriage work is even more powerful for our marriages—because our marriages matter the most.

Right now, you may be wondering if I'm from a marriage fantasy land with unicorns and rainbows because you are struggling with real issues. But I promise you there is an unbelievable power in living out the answer to the question . . .

What am I doing to make this marriage work?

What am I doing to make this marriage work?

When I was driving home from my 10th retreat for couples with children who have autism, I was hit with great clarity. I asked myself, "What is the difference between the couple whose marriage is barely surviving and the couple whose marriage is thriving?"

I realized it's not as much about the severity of the autism, and all that comes with it.
I realized it's not income.
It's not therapies.
It's not outside help.

The common denominator for the thriving couples was a mindset. They were on each other's team. They served each other. They appreciated each other. They gave each other breaks. They made time together. They communicated to their spouse their love and appreciation for each other.

They practiced what they promised.

After hearing their stories over and over, I thought, if these couples can have great marriages in the middle of the challenge and frustration, so can I, so can you. And I believe with my whole heart that marriage is easier than we have been led to believe, especially when we become intentional about doing a few things well—habits that are a part of our everyday interactions.

Have Serious Fun,
Love God First,
Respect and Love, and
Practice Your Promise.

While these habits may not always be easy to live out, they are easy to understand. And when they become habits in your marriage, your US can be better than you ever imagined.

God designed marriage to be great. You can do this, one step, one moment, one habit at time. Enjoy your marriage, and enjoy each other. Enjoy becoming your best US.

Appendix A: Negative Responses

Withdrawal: You avoid others or alienate yourself without resolution; you sulk or use the silent treatment.

Escalation: Your emotions spiral out of control; you argue, raise your voice, and fly into a rage.

Earn-it mode: You try to do more to earn others' love and care.

Negative beliefs: You believe your spouse is far worse than is really the case; you attribute negative motives to your spouse.

Blaming: You place responsibility on others, not accepting fault; you're convinced the problem is your spouse's fault.

Exaggeration: You make overstatements and enlarge your words beyond the bounds of the truth.

Tantrums: You have a fit of bad temper.

Denial: You refuse to admit the truth or reality.

Invalidation: You devalue your spouse; you do not appreciate who your partner is, what he or she feels or thinks or does.

Defensiveness: Instead of listening, you defend yourself by trying to provide an explanation.

Clinginess: You develop a strong emotional attachment or dependence on your spouse.

Passive-aggression: You display negative emotions, resentment, and aggression in unassertive passive ways, such as procrastination and stubbornness.

Caretaking: You become responsible for others by giving physical or emotional care and support to the point you are doing everything for your spouse and your partner does nothing to care for him or herself.

Acting out: You engage in negative behaviors or addictions like drug or alcohol abuse, extramarital affairs, excessive shopping or spending, or overeating.

Fix-it mode: You focus almost exclusively on what is needed to solve the problem.

Complaining/criticism: You express unhappiness or make accusations; you present a "laundry list" of faults about your mate.

Striking out: You become verbally or physically aggressive, possibly abusive.

Manipulation: You pursue your mate to get them to do what you want; you control your spouse for your own advantage.

Anger or rage: You display strong feelings of displeasure or violent and uncontrolled behavior.

Catastrophizing: You use dramatic, exaggerated expectations to depict that the relationship is in danger or that it has failed.

Emotional shutdown: You numb out emotionally; you become devoid of emotion, or you have no regard for others' needs or troubles.

Humor: You use humor as a way of not dealing with the issue at hand.

Sarcasm: You use negative humor, hurtful words, belittling comments, cutting remarks, or demeaning statements.

Minimization: You assert that your spouse is overreacting to an issue; you intentionally underestimate, downplay, or soft-pedal the issue.

Rationalization: You attempt to make your actions seem reasonable, you try to attribute your behavior to credible motives; you try to provide believable but untrue reasons for your conduct.

Indifference: You are cold and show no concern.

Abdication: You give away responsibilities.

Self-abandonment: You desert yourself; you neglect yourself; you run yourself down.

Appendix B: Negative Feelings

Rejected: My spouse doesn't want me; my spouse doesn't need me; my spouse does not desire me. I feel unwanted.

Abandoned: I will be alone; my spouse will ultimately leave me; I will be left alone to care for myself; my spouse won't be committed to me for life.

Disconnected: We will become emotionally detached or separated.

Like a failure: I am not successful at being a husband/wife; I will not perform rightly or correctly; I will not live up to expectations; I will fall short in our relationship; I am not good enough.

Helpless/powerless: I cannot do anything to change my situation. I do not possess the power, resources, capacity, or ability to get what I want. My spouse will control me.

Defective: Something is wrong with me; I'm the problem.

Inadequate: I am not capable; I am incompetent.

Inferior: Everyone else is better than I am; I am less valuable or important than others.

Invalidated: Who I am, what I think, what I do, or how I feel is not valued.

Unloved: My spouse doesn't love me anymore; my spouse has no affection or desire for me; my relationship lacks warm attachment, admiration, enthusiasm, or devotion; I feel as if we are just roommates and that there are no romantic feelings between us.

Dissatisfied: I will not experience satisfaction within the relationship; in our marriage, I will exist in misery for the rest of my life; I will not be pleased within my marriage; I feel no joy in my relationship.

Cheated: My spouse will take advantage of me; my spouse will withhold something I need; I won't get what I want.

Worthless/devalued: I am useless; I have no value to my spouse. I don't measure up. I am never able to meet my spouse's expectations of me; I am not good enough as a spouse.

Unaccepted: My spouse does not accept me; my spouse is not pleased with me; my spouse does not approve of me.

Notes

1. Andy Stanley's method is communicated in the following book: Stanley, Andy and Lane Jones. *Communicating for a Change: Seven Keys to Irresistible Communication*. Multnomah, 2008.

2. MarriedPeople creates resources that help churches help marriages with a proactive strategy. For more information about MarriedPeople, visit www.MarriedPeople.org.

3. Edwards, Scott. "Love and the Brain." The Harvard Mahoney Neuroscience Institute Letter. http://neuro.hms.harvard.edu/harvard-mahoney-neuroscience-institute/brain-newsletter/and-brain-series/love-and-brain.

4. That book has already been written. Check out *Parenting Beyond Your Capacity* by Reggie Joiner and Carey Nieuwhof (Orange Books).

5. Duhigg, Charles. *The Power of Habit: Why We Do What We Do in Life and Business*. Random House Trade Paperbacks, 2014.

6. Gottman, John M., Ph.D and Nan Silver. *The Seven Principles for Making Marriage Work*. Three Rivers Press, 1999.

7. Van Boven, Leaf. "Experientialism, Materialism, and the Pursuit of Happiness." *Review of General Psychology,* (2005) 9 (2), pp. 132-142

8. Johnson, Sue Ph.D. *Hold Me Tight: Seven Conversations for a Lifetime of Love*. Little, Brown and Company, 2008.

9. *Shadowlands*, directed by Richard Attenborough, performance by Anthony Hopkins, Home Box Office Video (USA), 1993

10. Mills, Harry, Ph.D. "Physiology of Anger." *MentalHelp.net*. https://www.mentalhelp.net/articles/physiology-of-anger/

11. Love, Patricia, Ed.D. and Steve Stosny, Ph.D. *How to Improve Your Marriage Without Talking About It: Finding Love Beyond Words*. Broadway, 2007.

12. For information about this organization, visit http://mylesapart.org.

13. Peterson, Karen S. "The Good in Bad Marriage." *USA Today*. 2001. http://usatoday30.usatoday.com/news/health/2001-06-21-divorce-usat.htm

14. Love, Patricia, Ed.D. and Steve Stosny, Ph.D. *How to Improve Your Marriage Without Talking About It: Finding Love Beyond Words*. Broadway, 2007.